D1223393

THE
Mayflower
AND OTHER COLONIAL VESSELS

Mayflower II *under sail, 1957.* (Plimoth Plantation, Inc)

THE
Mayflower
AND OTHER COLONIAL VESSELS

by

WILLIAM A BAKER

Naval Institute Press

© W A Baker 1983
First published in Great Britain in 1983 by Conway Maritime Press Ltd,
24 Bride Lane, Fleet St, London EC4Y 8DR.

Published and distributed in the United States of America and Canada
by the Naval Institute Press, Annapolis, Maryland 21402

Library of Congress Catalog Card No. 83-60472

ISBN 0-87021-843-3

Manufactured in the United Kingdom

Contents

Author's Note
and Acknowledgements

In the hustle, bustle, and uncertainties of late twentieth-century living in the United States more and more attention is being given to its history. This attention is being focused on restorations and reconstructions that tell visually of the technical abilities of the early settlers and their descendants and show how they lived and worked – and played if there was any time left.

Far-seeing people have recreated the glories of Virginia's colonial capital, Williamsburg; Connecticut has turned toward the sea with its Mystic Seaport; and Massachusetts has Plimoth Plantation and Sturbridge Village. Other restorations and reconstructions too numerous to list are scattered far and wide across the country.

Since the 1950s there has been a growing interest in the preservation of old ships and small craft on both coasts, the Great Lakes, and the great rivers. Obviously vessels of the early colonial days are not available for preservation – no American *Wasa* is likely to be found – but to show what they were like a number of replicas or reproductions have been built. This book, which incorporates material from two long out-of-print books, describes a few such vessels with which I have been associated. I do not know enough about those by other designers in the United States, the United Kingdom, and Europe to be able to comment on them.

The designing of the new *Mayflower* was for me a form of 'busman's holiday' as she was created during my spare time while employed as a naval architect by a large shipbuilding company. As an avocation I had studied for many years all manner of things concerning old ships hence her design was based on sound technical material from the sixteenth and seventeenth centuries tempered where necessary by modern engineering knowledge. I must acknowledge the work of all who have delved into the history of the original *Mayflower* and the design, construction and rigging of seventeenth century ships. Without

AUTHOR'S NOTES

their studies my job would have been well nigh impossible. Their names are legion but many will be found in the text and in the foot-note references.

In a different way I must acknowledge very gratefully the efforts of those who faithfully translated my plans into living vessels: Stuart A Upham and all hands at the yard of J W & A Upham Ltd, Brixham, Devon, England; George S Davis and the men of the Plymouth Marine Railways, Inc, Plymouth, Massachusetts; the late Captain Ralph McCallon and his helpers of St Georges, Bermuda; and James B Richardson and those working in his yard at Lloyds, Dorchester County, Maryland.

My thanks go to the Editors of *The American Neptune* for permission to use material published therein; to Plimoth Plantation, Inc, for permission to publish the sail plan of the new *Mayflower* and the lines of the *Pilgrim Shallop II*; to the late Mr M V Brewington for perusing some of the pinnace material; and to the late Mr H I Chapelle for comments concerning ketches.

Special credit must go to my wife for correcting and typing the manuscript, for compiling the glossary, for typing the specifications and keeping the correspondence flowing during the construction of the various vessels, and for her persistence in keeping the text somewhat intelligible to one not having a full technical background.

W A Baker

Introduction

When the first European colonists landed along the Atlantic seaboard of North America they faced a trackless forest, trackless save for a few Indian trails with which they would have to become acquainted. There were no roads, no carriages, and not even any horses. Behind them was the even greater trackless waste that they had just crossed, the sea which would serve them as a primary means of communication and as one source of food.

Considering the importance of the sea to the new settlements, knowledge of the maritime activities of their inhabitants is relatively meager. True, there are official records, letters and other documents listing vessels owned here and there, describing certain exploring and trading trips and mentioning fishing and other pursuits, but there must have been far more activity than that covered by the preserved material. There is little describing the vessels employed which were the trucks and buses of their day. This condition stems from the fact that all such activities and the vessels themselves were so common-place to the settlers that complete records and detailed descriptions were not thought necessary. It was only the unusual that attracted attention.

While people have always sought information about the vessels that carried the early colonists to North America there is at present more than a passing interest in colonial-built craft. Any study of the types of vessels employed in colonial North American shipping can assume certain vessel characteristics deriving from the national backgrounds of the colonists. The region that became New York was obviously Dutch. This influence was also strong along the Delaware River where too could be found Swedish and, somewhat later, German settlements. Colonists in New England, Maryland, Virginia, the Carolinas and Georgia would have built vessels similar to those that they had known in England. The French were not unknown along the coast of what became the State of Maine and the Maritime Provinces of Canada while Spanish-type vessels were constructed in Florida.

English and other national fishing fleets – Biscayners were well known to seamen – had been coming to the north-eastern coast of the present United States, Nova Scotia, and Newfoundland for years before permanent settlements were established. Their experiences must have had some influence on the types and details of vessels built in the New World or sent out from the mother countries in Europe.

The majority of the colonies that eventually became the United States, however, were English or were taken over by England; hence this study of vessels that carried colonists and those built in the colonies will be limited generally to English types. It must be recognized, though, that because of the extensive North Sea and cross-Channel trades there always was some maritime influence from one country to another in northern Europe. Thus the deep-sea merchant ships tended to be of a few universal types with perhaps certain features modified by local conditions such as the shallow waters off the Netherlands and at the entrance to the Baltic. Vessels employed solely in domestic commerce and fishing generally preserved their national characteristics.

Two sources for type names of English vessels of the early seventeenth century are the charters granted the shipwrights in 1605 and 1612. The 1605 charter named the group as the 'Master, Wardens and Commonalty of the Art or Mystery of Shipwrights of England' and listed the types of vessels over which it had jurisdiction as 'ships and barges ship's boats pinnaces and like vessels'. This charter was withdrawn and a new one granted in 1612 was much more explicit concerning the floating equipment encompassed: 'ships, carvels, hoys, pinnaces, crayers, ketches, lighters, boats, barges, wherries or any other vessel or vessels whatsoever'. The types named included those employed in the normal domestic and overseas trades; presumably the multitude of fishing vessel types was covered by the last six words.

These charters, coming as they did at the dawn of the English settlement of the New World, named most of the floating equipment available to the early colonists. From the accounts of voyages recorded by Richard Hakluyt and Samuel Purchas we can add hulks, flyboats, clinchers, barks, frigates, galleys, and brigantines. English colonial records list shallops, pinks, galliots, bateaux, flats, punts, piraguas, and – often qualified in the earliest records as 'Dutch' – sloops, in addition to many of those previously mentioned.

INTRODUCTION

When attempting to trace the history and development of any type of vessel, three main features should be considered: form, construction and rig. As the rig of a vessel is the most apparent feature this category has been popular with the average researcher and nautical enthusiast. Studies of form run a poor second while construction is rarely mentioned, probably because of the scarcity of information and the fact that details changed but slowly as time passed.

It is difficult to convince the average nautical enthusiast that, until the mid-nineteenth century, rig had little connection with the designation of ship or boat types. Size, form, construction or other considerations usually determined the type name. Classification by rig alone, while convenient in some circumstances, is akin to describing modern fishing boats by the type of internal combustion motor installed – a Cape Unknown lobsterman has a Ford conversion but a Blank Harbor dragger must have a Penta diesel – which tells little or nothing of the boats themselves. It is true that with the passing of time, certain rigs became associated with specific hull forms for special employment such as fishing, coastal trading, river work and the like, but these are rather recent developments in history.

Among other influences that led to certain type names are the use or place of use, an unusual feature, the name of the first vessel of the type, or even a world event. The French 'chasse-marie'; the Dutch 'boyer'; the American 'Block Island boat', 'sharpie', and 'bugeye'; the English 'boomie' and 'Una-boat'; and the Scottish 'zulu' are typical. The terms 'lobsterman' and 'dragger' used above, 'collier', 'tanker', and 'lumber schooner' are present day examples of use giving a type name, none of which gives any indication of the size, shape, construction or rig of a vessel.

The foregoing and similar names meant something distinct to the vessels' employers, referring to specific types of vessels by which they earned their livings, but the names meant little or nothing to others. Certainly many of the ancient terms are enigmas to mid-twentieth-century researchers. Some type definitions have changed so radically with the passing years that it is almost impossible to trace them back to the seventeenth century. Other types are not even noted in the earliest marine dictionaries; these may be examples of 'use' names not thought necessary to define. Still others may be synonymous or may be defining the hull and rig of the same vessel. Bits of information, however, may be gleaned from here and there and, piece by piece, some reasonably convincing portraits of many seventeenth-century vessel types can be assembled.

THE MAYFLOWER

The characteristics of a vessel of an earlier period can be presented in three ways and the effectiveness of the result depends largely on the medium chosen. Obviously, the simplest is two-dimensional, that is, by means of a drawing, etching or painting. Many details can be shown but much is hidden or can only be suggested. Unless the viewpoint chosen is unusual nothing can be shown of the deck arrangements and it is difficult to give an idea of hull shape. On the other hand, the rigging and sails can be shown with considerable accuracy. In the main, however, an artist is concerned with creating a feeling of the vessel and in showing the items that readily meet the eye – the sweep of the sheer line and rails, the details of decoration, the set of the sails, the condition of the sea, and the play of light on all.

From a technical point of view a three-dimensional model is a more satisfactory method. The shape of the under- and above-water portions of the hull can be shown as well as the arrangements of the weather decks, many of the interesting fittings, and all the spars and rigging. Sails are generally but clumsy additions unless the model be large enough to have the material of which they are made of the proper scale thickness. Models may seem somewhat lifeless compared with many drawings and paintings but they give a feeling of form and mass that cannot be had from two-dimensional portrayals.

Neither an artist's conception nor a model, however, can convey adequately the impression of the mass of an actual vessel, or the size of the equipment, and of the space available for living and working. A number of vessels of various periods are being preserved to give those interested some knowledge of form, construction, rigging, and of how people lived and worked on board. When no suitable examples are available for preservation there has been a growing interest since the end of World War II in the building of reproductions. 'Replica' is a simpler word but it implies more accuracy than is often warranted. I have been involved in the design and construction of a number of these which will be discussed in the following chapters.

CHAPTER 1

Seventeenth-Century Naval Architecture

A. GENERAL

Before considering specific re-creations of vessels a brief outline of the state of the art of naval architecture in the seventeenth century is needed to make the subsequent material more intelligible. Naval architects, in the modern sense of ship designers who may have no connection with a shipyard, did not exist except in the rare case of what might be called an interested amateur. Generally speaking, each master builder designed the vessels he built using long established rules for proportions, scantlings, and rig which, under normal circumstances, produced vessels similar to those that had proved satisfactory in service. Changes were small from vessel to vessel but over a long period definite trends could be observed, the result of changes in trade patterns that altered cargo carrying requirements, refinements of form, improvements in rig, availability of timber, and mere whim and fashion.

Since almost the beginning of maritime history there have been two classes of seagoing vessels. Until the advent of mechanical means of propulsion there were those propelled by oars – the classic 'long' ship, the galley used for war and services requiring speed, and those propelled by sails – the classic 'round' ship employed for commerce. As time passed, there were many attempts to combine the advantages of each with but little success except in a few special cases. The use of rowers on a trading vessel, apart from the space they occupied, required great stocks of food and water that reduced the space available for cargo. The bulkier vessels that resulted from increasing the sail power and cargo capacity of the galley type made for poor performance under oars. The great merchant galleys of Venice were notable exceptions but they were successful only when carrying the high value, low bulk cargoes of silks and spices from the East.

In addition to the seagoing types of merchant vessels suitable for long voyages there was a multitude of smaller vessels employed for coastwise trading, river work and fishing. Some were miniature versions of the seagoing types; others had unique characteristics to suit their special conditions of employment. Before discussing some of these we must define the form, construction and rig of a typical early seventeenth century merchant *ship*.

In the very use of the simple word 'ship' we are in the middle of a classification confusion, for the term was employed in both the general and specific senses. Turning for the moment to the current Webster's *New International Dictionary* we can find under 'ship' the following:

1. Any large seagoing vessel.
2. Specific, *Naut*, a vessel with a bowsprit and three masts (foremast, mainmast, and mizzenmast), with, rarely, a fourth mast, each composed of a lower mast, a topmast, and a topgallantmast, and, sometimes, higher masts; all masts being square rigged.

Here we have the general and specific definitions with the latter representing the final version of the sail-propelled 'round ship', a definition based on rig alone which became the fashion during the nineteenth century. Since the introduction of this type of definition we can find in nineteenth-century literature repeated references to packet ships, clipper ships, cotton ships, whaling ships, etc, which gave the knowledgeable some inkling as to size, shape and construction. Generally speaking, the word 'ship' designated the highest class of sailing vessel.

Throughout recorded history there has been at any given time some particular type of vessel that was the 'ship' of its period, the highest development at that time. Starting no further back than medieval times there were cogs, nefs, hulks, carracks, and, by the early seventeenth century, the galleon which was intimately associated with Spain and the flute, a Dutch type. Such names came into being because trade conditions and fashion changed sufficiently to lead to the development of a vessel different enough from the current 'ship' to warrant a new type name. In spite of the building of new types the old ones would have held on for a considerable period hence, at any given time, there would have been several types of large vessels that a sailor would have classed as a 'ship'. In any of the basic types there were certain national characteristics by which it was possible to recognize the vessels of each of the major seafaring countries.

Because of vagaries in language some type names have caused considerable trouble for marine researchers. A type name originating in one country would be adopted with slight modification by a second, this in turn changed by a third, and so on. The modern researcher then tries to define several types between which there is no basic difference. The converse is also true, the same name being employed in northern Europe and the Mediterranean region for vastly different types of vessels.

To see what vessel types would have been familiar to a colonist in one of the English North American settlements, let us examine an early seventeenth-century port scene. J C Visscher's 1616 view of London as seen from the south bank of the River Thames is a convenient example. This view covers the river from the bend at Whitehall on the west to slightly below the Tower on the east with the old London Bridge separating the seagoing vessels from the up-stream craft. Looking at the sailing vessels, those up-river to the west of the bridge are local types that could pass under the bridge by lowering their masts; there are also three larger vessels that had been built or re-rigged there. Below the bridge are various fore-and-aft and square-rigged vessels, coasters and deep-sea types. In all Visscher showed at least seventy-nine rigged vessels of various types and, in addition, many oar-propelled craft ranging from hay barges to State barges.

Starting with the simplest sailing type, there are eight small craft carrying but a single square sail. Next come small open boats, both double-enders and those with transom sterns, rigged with one mast carrying a sprit mainsail and a staysail. There are over a dozen of these above the bridge and at least eight below. Larger vessels with the same rig but having shelters over their cargo holds are shown below the bridge; two of these are double-enders and three have the small high transom or 'pink' stern.

Easily identified east of the bridge are at least five hoys, large fore-and-aft rigged coasting and cross-Channel vessels that carried a sprit mainsail, a staysail, and a square topsail. Although bowsprits are shown hoys probably did not have jibs at this early date but may have carried a small square sail under their bowsprits. Two 'eell schipes' are shown moored above the bridge off Queenhithe near St Paul's church; for centuries Dutch fishing interests had the right to keep these receiving vessels in the Thames. Modern versions of these eel ships, not changed much at that, could be seen in the river until shortly after World War I. The 1616 vessels are rigged with a staysail forward, a sprit main, and a small sprit mizzen. As for square-rigged seagoing vessels, there are about forty of various sizes, all carrying the normal 'ship' rig of the period. This rig had three masts, the fore and main being square rigged, the mizzen having a single lateen sail, and there was a square sail under the bowsprit. Examples of most of these types

3

from the 1616 print are shown in Fig 1.

Using the 1612 Shipwrights' charter as a guide, can we name the types shown in the 1616 view of London? Strictly from the rig point of view the answer in general is 'no'. Some of the seagoing square-riggers obviously must be 'ships' because they are the largest vessels shown. Carvels (or caravels) were a southern European type employed chiefly by the Portuguese and Spanish which could easily be identified by their rig of two or more lateen sails; none are shown. Hoys we have definitely noted above; these were easily-handled shallow-draft vessels fitted with leeboards and the one-masted rig described. Of the remainder – 'pinnaces, crayers, ketches, lighters, boats, barges, wherries. . .' – we cannot name them by rig alone and we must assume that the types required certain form and construction characteristics as well.

1. *Vessels at London, 1616 – after Visscher*

SEVENTEENTH-CENTURY NAVAL ARCHITECTURE

B. RIG

Continuing our discussion of the 1616 view of London we can see from the vessels described and shown in Fig 1 that there was no great variety of rig. The fore-and-aft and the square rig are fitted on both large and small vessels. Views of other ports, however, do show a few other rigs and there are many paintings and prints available that depict fishing and other local craft, particularly of Dutch types that were copied widely in the countries bordering the North Sea. It will be noted that, apart from the 'eell schipes', there are no two-masted vessels in the 1616 print. Other evidence indicates that during the seventeenth century there were many vessels of all sizes, some as long as 100ft on deck, rigged with two masts carrying various combinations of fore-and-aft and square sails. Basically these rigs were like that of the hoy with a small lateen mizzen added, the forerunners of the ketch rig. And I believe that a two-masted square rig was employed more extensively than evidence such as the 1616 view indicates.

We have mentioned the forty or so 'ship' rigged vessels, about half the total number of sailing vessels shown; possibly some of these are as small as 45ft in length on deck, incredible as it may seem. The large number is a direct result of the popularity of the hoy rig, or hoy plus lateen mizzen. England depended on a reservoir of trained merchant seamen for the manning of her fighting ships in time of war. Because the hoy rig was so handy, vessels so rigged had smaller crews than those carrying the normal ship rig and it was feared that there would be a shortage of trained men. In 1558, a Navigation Act prohibited any English hoy or plate, a vessel similarly rigged but of even shallower draft, from trading to continental ports on the penalty of forfeiture but did allow such trading by vessels with cross sails. This act was repealed in 1562 and hoys were allowed to trade with North Sea ports from Normandy to Norway. But because of 'the decay of Mariners and Ships by the marvellous increase of hoys' the law was reinstated in 1571; the date of its eventual repeal, if at all, is not available.

Not shown below the bridge in the 1616 view of London is the four-masted rig fitted on the largest royal and merchant ships; it was probably not carried on new ships later than the second decade of the seventeenth century. The fore- and mainmasts were square rigged but, as a single lateen sail would have been unwieldy on a large ship, two mizzen masts were stepped, the main mizzen and the bonaventure mizzen. Incidentally, the term 'mizzen' applied to a sail in the early seventeenth century always meant a lateen. When the bonaventure mizzen was finally abandoned a square topsail was fitted on the main mizzen mast over a relatively small lateen and the development of the ship rig with three square-rigged masts was started.

Some researchers have held that early colonial American ketches and pinnaces were rigged with lateen sails only. It seems strange, however, that if the lateen sail was employed widely on small vessels in early colonial days it would disappear so completely as not to be shown on similar vessels in early eighteenth-century views of Boston, New York, Philadelphia and other ports and then return to use after 1750. This is a convenient point at which to consider the problem.

Taking into account the backgrounds of the early Atlantic Coast colonists as noted in the Introduction, only the French in the north and the Spanish far to the south would without question have had first-hand common knowledge of the lateen rig. It was employed extensively for their local craft by the natives on the Mediterranean coasts of both France and Spain. If the other three countries – England, Holland and Sweden – used the lateen rig in any form for their small craft some pictorial evidence should be available.[1]

It might be argued that such pictorial evidence is unreliable and this may be so but at this late date little else is available. In certain early series of city views the same types of vessels were used indiscriminately for all parts of the world but in the seafaring nations that were sending out colonists there was considerable awareness of the maritime scene. A wrong type of vessel or a crude portrayal would jar the eyes of the knowledgeable viewer to the detriment of the artist's reputation. Still, one must choose one's artists carefully because all obviously were not at the same level of competence. A Mediterranean-type galley, although hardly suitable for service in the stormy English Channel and the North Sea, is acceptable in an early seventeenth century Dutch port scene because of the political situation in which the Low Countries and Spain were involved. The same type of vessel in an American scene would be absurd unless it could be proved that such a craft was built on the western shore of the Atlantic.

On the other hand artists took all sorts of liberties in their portrayals of cities and countries overseas. Public interest in foreign ports was high and prints apparently were snapped up regardless of accuracy which, of course, the public had no means of checking. A prize example of this is a 1672 print titled 'Nowel Amsterdam en L'Amerique'. At the time Manhattan had been known to the Dutch for over fifty years and reasonably accurate maps and other views existed. This print, however, is pure fantasy and is based on a view of Lisbon that may be dated between 1576 and 1618. The vessels in the 'Nowel Amsterdam' version follow those depicted in the Lisbon print and include a typical Mediterranean galley and lateen-rigged caravels.[2]

Turning now to our pictorial evidence, Visscher's 1616 London had been described. The only lateen sails shown are the mizzens on the square-rigged vessels, none at all on any small craft. A similar analysis was made of seven other representative English, Dutch and Scandinavian port scenes; more are available but there is no need to pile up numbers. It is sufficient to say that apart from the lateen mizzens on the square-riggers there are but three lateen-rigged vessels in a total of over three hundred. These three are typical Mediterranean galleys shown at Amsterdam and Rotterdam which, as noted earlier, is not surprising. On the basis of vessels employed in their home waters it seems reasonable to conclude that the English, Dutch, and Swedes would not have used a lateen rig on the local fishing and trading craft built in their New World colonies.

To strengthen further this conclusion with respect to the English use of lateen sails is the statement of Sir Henry Mainwaring concerning 'carvells':[3]

> Carvels are vessels which go with mizen-sails [ie lateen sails] instead of mainsails [ie square sails]. They have three mizens: the main mizen, which belongs to the mainmast; the after mizen and bonaventure mizen as in some of the King's ships; but they have foremast and boltsprit rigged in every sort like other ships. These will be nearer the wind than cross sails, *but are not so commodious to handle. We have here little use of them and therefore I speak not much. . .*
> (Parenthetical notes and italics added by the author).

Mainwaring was describing, of course, the well-known *caravela redonda* widely employed by the Portuguese. In northern European waters and around the coasts of the British Isles where shifting winds, strong tidal currents, and many rivers required handy vessels the lateen rig was just not convenient hence the widespread use of the simple fore-and-aft rig. We can not deny that an occasional ketch or pinnace may have carried a lateen rig but the common rigs of small colonial North American vessels will be discussed in the chapters to follow.

C. FORM AND CONSTRUCTION

Apart from purely local flat-bottomed craft, shipbuilders of the early seventeenth century were limited to two basic forms of sailing vessels, what may best be called the 'ship' form and the 'boat' form. The ship form was that employed for the great trading and fighting galleons and for the smaller vessels that aped their characteristics. One distinguishing feature was a flat transom stern that may be seen on most portrayals of square-rigged vessels of the period. Apart from the visual evidence offered by paintings and prints that the same form was employed for various sizes of vessels, there is one drawing dating from about the last quarter of the sixteenth century that shows the profile and several sections of a ship with five different scales.[4] Standardized ships are not a twentieth-century invention.

In contrast to the square-sterned ship form the boat form was double-ended but sometimes so blunt that any relationship to such fine-lined vessels as those built by the Vikings might be doubted. It could be and was built in various sizes in the same manner as the ship form. In northern Europe a great variety of large and small fishing and trading vessels had the double-ended boat form. Perhaps the best known example of a large double-ender was the tubby Dutch 'fluyt' (flute).

During the centuries of slow progress in ship design and construction that followed man's first venture afloat on a log, the shape of vessels departed but gradually from the basic proportions of the hollowed-out log canoe, the ancestor of the boat form. The oar-propelled vessels remained nearly true double-enders to the end of their days but the form of sailing vessels went through many changes; as the shape of their sections changed from the rough semi-circle of the log, decks, and eventually superstructures, were added.

About the middle of the fifteenth century the shape of sailing vessels' sterns was changed from a full rounding type to a flat transom. The new stern gave better support to the after superstructures and allowed the shipwright to mold them into the hull proper. The superstructures of medieval ships were definitely additions rather than integral parts, light rectangular buildings erected by house carpenters on the strong curved work of the shipwrights. The two types of sterns are shown in Fig 2.

From the hydrodynamic point of view, however, the flat transom was poorer than the medieval round stern as it caused considerable drag and made for poor steering. A fair portion of the rudder was operating in the eddy behind the hull and hence was ineffective. To improve steering one treatise recommended that the after edge of the rudder be made thicker than the forward edge, a detail that may be found on rudders of some modern tug-boats when extra control is required. In English ships, starting about 1650, the lower portion of the stern was rounded to reduce the drag but the upper section remained flat. Although this form of stern eventually was adopted by the major seafaring nations, it distinguished English ships for several decades.

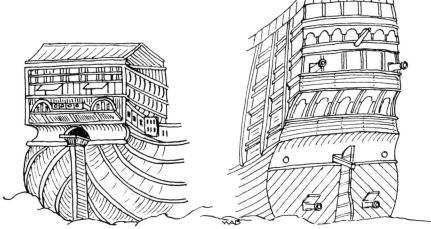

2. Fifteenth-century round stern and sixteenth-century transom stern

It is commonly believed that shipbuilders in olden times first carved half-hull models from which they took the measurements needed to build their ships. Designing by model alone was a rather decadent practice of the nineteenth century but as long as the vessels did not change radically many clever builders were able to obtain good results. Actually, by the seventeenth century, the major builders did a fair amount of drawing. Not, to be sure, in the modern fashion with nearly every nut and bolt depicted but enough to establish the basic proportions and shape, the extent of superstructures, and often the hull decorations. There is a record of a plan being sent out from England in 1638 for the construction of a small vessel in Massachusetts.

Some extant Italian drawings of ship parts date back to the first half of the fifteenth century. During the sixteenth century the leaders in the field of naval architecture were the master shipwrights of the great Mediterranean ports such as Genoa and Venice and the shipwrights of northern Europe followed their lead. Henry VIII of England actually brought Italian shipwrights to England to help build up his fleet.

Through the ages shipbuilding knowledge was normally passed on from a master shipwright to his apprentices. By the beginning of the seventeenth century much had been committed to writing and is now

THE MAYFLOWER

preserved in the form of notebooks or manuscript treatises. The Baker MS cited earlier in a footnote is one such notebook which has material on the design, construction, and sparring of vessels ranging from those in the fleet of Henry VIII to proposals of about 1600. Mathew Baker was a master shipwright of the first Queen Elizabeth. By the mid-seventeenth century several useful books on shipbuilding had been printed. In most of the early manuscripts and the books that followed many details of the design procedure were omitted. They were either assumed to be common knowledge or were such trade secrets that no shipwright would part with them. It is impossible for us today to comprehend fully some of the design procedure and to know what is meant by certain terms.

Ships of the late sixteenth and early seventeenth centuries had definite shape characteristics quite apart from the prominent decorative features so apparent in their portraits. The underbody, normally hidden from view, had full rounding curves while the relatively straight topside tumbled home to high narrow decks. These shape characteristics were the direct results of the design methods that made extensive use of arcs of circles. A ship's sections were composed of several arcs drawn with a pair of compasses while large radius fore-and-aft arcs were calculated mathematically or worked out to a close approximation by a simple mechanical method.

Of great importance in the design of any vessel was the shape of the largest section and its location with respect to the length of the keel. Although for convenience it was usually called the 'midship bend' (frame) it was normally located about one-third of the length of the keel from its forward end. The widest part of this section was just above the load waterline. The point of maximum breadth was raised progressively towards the ends of the ship to improve seaworthiness by providing extra buoyancy and to give finer sections below for easy passage through the water. The above location of the midship bend gave a vessel a full bow and a fine stern in keeping with the long held theory that a good ship should have a 'cod's head and a mackerel's tail'. One drawing in the Baker MS shows the outline of a fish super-imposed on the underwater profile of a ship.

1. *Detail of ¼in scale model of the* Mayflower (*rigged by E A R Ronnberg*)

10

THE MAYFLOWER

Fig 3 shows the method of drawing the outline of the midship bend for a typical late sixteenth- or early seventeenth-century ship. First, a rectangle is drawn using the chosen breadth and depth of the proposed ship, the depth being the height of the maximum breadth above the top of the keel which was used as the base line. Subtract one-fifth of the half breadth ED from the depth which locates point G and draw HG parallel to the base. Next draw a line from E to C intersecting HG at J and through this point erect KM perpendicular to the base; EK is the half breadth of the floor. Set off HL at two-thirds of ED. With a compass find point N on KM so that an arc tangent to the base will pass through L. On an extension of the line LN find the center O for the arc LC. The third center Q on OC is found by drawing a line from P through N. Point R which determines the tumble home of the topside is two-thirds of the half-breadth from the centerline and twice the height of Q above the base. It will be noticed that because of the location of point Q the actual breadth and depth of the vessel will be slightly greater than the dimensions chosen for the basic rectangle. The section shown is relatively simple; others of the period had an additional arc in the body while the topsides often had a reverse curve so that they were nearly vertical at the weather deck.

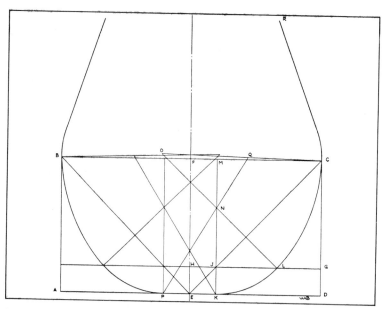

3. *Outline of typical midsection of an early seventeenth-century ship*

The process of drawing the lines plan started with the setting down to a convenient scale on paper – or perhaps a smooth plank – a profile or side view showing the outlines of the keel, stem, and sternpost. The length of straight keel that 'treads the ground' was one of the basic measurements of a ship. The forward curve of the stem plus the rake aft of the sternpost usually about equalized the maximum breadth. Next the outline of the midship bend was drawn at its proper location on the keel. Starting from this midship bend and working toward the bow and stern it is obvious that the area of each successive section must be progressively smaller if the vessel is to have a reasonable shape. The amount of reduction for each section was guided by fore-and-aft lines showing the maximum breadth and floor line both in plan and profile, the so-called narrowing and rising lines. Originally these were arcs of circles of large radius but later they became mathematically derived curves.

The narrowing and rising lines for the floor show how far its center must move inboard and rise in order to produce the proper form. At the ends and particularly forward the narrowing line might actually cross the centerline in which case the floor arc was not part of the frame outline but served only to guide the bottom of the body sweep. The location and shape of the narrowing and rising lines for the maximum breadth determined whether a ship was chunky or fine. An easily curved narrowing line forward and a rising line that was much higher at the ends than at the midship bend produced a relatively fine and speedy hull. Blunting the forward end of the narrowing line and dropping the ends of the rising line made a tubbier ship, slower than the previous one but capable of carrying a heavier armament if a warship or more cargo if a merchantman.

By employing the narrowing and rising lines any transverse section of the ship could be drawn with a compass and a straightedge. Available information indicates that the outlines of sections so drawn were transferred directly to the timbers chosen for any particular frame. Shipwrights of the period apparently had no knowledge of the process of fairing a set of ship's lines by waterlines and buttocks. Reference to Fig 4 may help to clarify this brief outline of the design procedures.

By 1600 the use of the cargo carrying capacity of a ship as a basis for assessing port charges and duties on imports and exports was an old practice. Medieval methods of determining this capacity are not known but by the same date the maritime nations generally employed some simple formula that involved a ship's length, breadth and depth, all

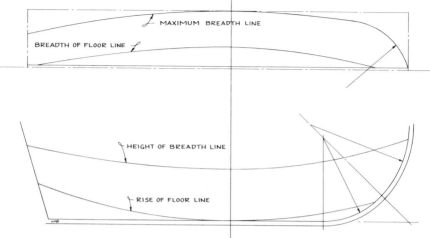

4. Narrowing and rising lines

measured in different ways by each country. Usually a suitable divisor appeared in the formula to bring theory into line with what an average ship actually could carry. The unit of capacity also varied but in England and France it was the Bordeaux wine cask or tun from which the modern term 'ton' is derived.

Again by 1600 the theoretical number of wine tuns that an English ship could stow in her hold, her 'burden', was given by:

$$\text{keel length} \times \text{breadth} \times \frac{\text{depth}}{100} = \text{tons burden.}$$

Generally these three dimensions were measured as noted earlier although from time to time variations were introduced in attempts to obtain better accuracy. Thus merchant ships were measured by their hold space only, that occupied by the crew and guns, the 'tween deck space, being excluded. Vessels hired by the Crown, however, were rated according to their entire internal capacity, their 'tons and tonnage', which usually was determined by increasing the burden by one-third. A ship having a burden of 150 tons had a tons and tonnage of 200 tons. As long as the decks within the hull maintained certain positions relative to the basic depth and the form followed established patterns, such tonnage formulas gave figures close to what the average ships actually carried.

After a ship was completed, however, it was difficult to measure the breadth and depth in the manner indicated. It became more or less

II. *The* Mayflower *model built by Anderson and Pritchard.* (Popperfoto)

common practice to take the maximum breadth to the outside of the planking and the depth from the height of breadth to the bottom of the keel. Now a single thickness of planking is a small percentage of the breadth and would not have much effect on the value of the burden but in cases where a ship's stability proved insufficient shipwrights added one or more layers of thick planking on the outside around the waterline, which was just about the widest part of a ship. This practice was known as 'furring' or 'girdling' and during the early seventeenth century it was said that more English ships were furred than those of any other nation. A burden calculated with a breadth measured to the outside of such furring was considerably larger than the number of tuns that could be stowed. In spite of such conditions and changes in ship design the above English formula remained in general use until 1694 but modifications were used at various ports during the second half of the seventeenth century.[5]

Although tonnages are available for all types of small craft we do not know exactly how they were determined. In using the English rule stated above the keel length and breadth offer no problems but for many small open craft that had vertical or nearly vertical sides there is a question as to what point was taken for the depth. It probably was measured from the top of the keel to the rail at its lowest point.

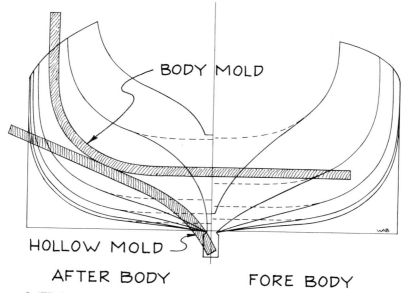

BODY MOLD

HOLLOW MOLD

AFTER BODY   FORE BODY

5. 'Whole-molding' of small boat hulls

The design procedure for open boats, and probably for small vessels too, was in theory the same as for the large ships. There were the usual narrowing and rising lines for breadth and floor but, instead of drawing the sections with a compass, two molds were used. Fig 5 illustrates the use of these molds better than several paragraphs of words; one mold shapes the topside and the other the reverse curve to the keel. The procedure was known as 'whole-molding'. In proper hands it could produce a fine-lined speedy hull as well as the more burdensome types with the assurance that, if the narrowing and rising lines were drawn as fair curves, the remainder of the hull would be fair with no special effort. Small boats that I have designed by this method have proved able and fast under sail.

Both procedures, the compass method and whole molding, would, if followed to the letter, fail to produce a fair form at the ends of a vessel. Here the art of the shipwright took precedence over the mechanical method of drawing. Further there would be local unfair spots or bumps particularly where arcs of greatly differing radii came tangent to each other. These look queer to modern eyes but are essential features of ships of the period. There is little doubt, however, that very pronounced bumps in the framing would have been removed by the shipwright's adz as soon as he found that he was having difficulty in fitting the planking.

Little definite manuscript or printed material is available concerning the arrangement and construction of late sixteenth- and early seventeenth-century ships but this situation improved with the passing of time. The excellent transcription of a manuscript of about 1620 on shipbuilding, published in 1958 by the Society for Nautical Research, filled out our knowledge considerably but most of our information must be pieced together from paintings and prints plus a few written descriptions.[6]

Considering the seagoing square-rigged ships in any of the port scenes and the single-ship portraits of the period we find that almost regardless of size the majority have certain features in common. At the forward end is a ram-like structure, the beakhead, protruding from the stem. The hull proper has a short superstructure forward, the forecastle, while the waist amidships is relatively low. A long high superstructure covers the after part of the hull from the mainmast to the stern; it usually had two levels but on some large ships there were three. Practically all the ships are armed; gunports show in the sides of all but the smallest.

The elaborate superstructures are a carry-over from the days when the art of gunnery was not well developed. It was customary to attack a ship by boarding and the defenders fought back level by level in the same manner that a castle on land would have been defended. The forecastle is the lineal descendant of the old fighting platform that actually looked much like a turret on a castle. Similarly the longer superstructure aft is a development of the 'after-castle' or 'summer-castle' that served originally as a command post and as a shelter for important persons carried as passengers.

The fore- and after-castles long remained little more than light angular structures. The earliest were platforms supported on stanchions above the weather deck; later, to provide shelter, the spaces below the platforms were enclosed with sheathing. Such superstructures could easily be swept overboard in a gale and, as they increased in size, a better method of securing them to the hull was required. The system generally adopted was to fit heavy vertical tie timbers on the outside extending well down on the main hull. During the first half of the sixteenth century the framing of the superstructures became an extension of that of the main hull.

By the early seventeenth century, the space within the forecastle was probably of more importance than the area of the forecastle deck that originally determined its worth as a fighting platform. Just how this space was equipped and employed, and indeed, exactly how any of the smaller spaces on shipboard were fitted out, is open to question. It is reasonable to assume that on ordinary merchant ships part of the forecastle space served as the galley or 'cook-room' which in naval vessels long remained in the hold or on a lower deck.

People having some knowledge of sailing ships are familiar with the so-called clipper bow – a clean concave profile with a simple carved figure – but few realize that it was the final development of the ram of the ancient war galley. The bow structures were originally termed 'beaks', then 'beakheads', and finally just 'heads'. The forecastle on medieval sailing ships, in its development from a simple fighting platform, came to have a triangular plan form with the pointed forward end projecting over the stemhead. As bowsprits increased in size and needed stronger steps in the hull they and the forecastle projections were lowered leaving a square forward bulkhead on the forecastle. The beakheads of the late sixteenth and early seventeenth centuries had more or less vertical sides with solid planking, a carry-over from the solid sides of the projecting forecastle. The sides were highly decorated and there was usually a grotesque head or some sort of a figure at the forward end. Often the upper profile was an S-curve, terminating near the top of the forecastle. With the passing of time the beakhead became shorter, higher, and lighter in appearance until the whole culminated in the bare clipper bow.

In the early seventeenth century the beakhead served several purposes in addition to decoration. It broke the seas before they could damage the forecastle, provided a solid structure to which the bowsprit

III. *Molds for* Mayflower II *laid out on the mold loft floor, November 1955.* (Author)

could be secured, and served as a place of convenience for the crew. A beakhead also served as a means of identification. Those on English ships were described as being long and low while on Spanish and Venetian ships, for example, the steeve, or angle with the baseline, of the beakheads was considerable.

The size and height of the after superstructure were often carried to such extremes as to affect seriously the seakeeping qualities of the ships. During the reign of the first Queen Elizabeth many noted seafarers inveighed against excessive superstructures but their recommendations usually were not heeded by those responsible for having the ships built. Sir Walter Raleigh stated that 'two decks and a half is sufficient to yield shelter for men and mariners and no more charging at all higher, but only one low cabbin for the master'.[7] The two decks are, of course, the lower or gundeck and the upper deck. The 'half' is the first level of the after superstructure extending from about the mainmast to the stern and called the 'halfdeck' because it covered about half the length of the vessel.

Under the halfdeck at the very stern was the 'great cabin' and just forward of this, separated by a bulkhead, was the helmsman's station, the 'steerage'. There was another bulkhead at the forward end of the steerage and a third, either full or partial, slightly forward of or just abaft the mainmast. On large warships the latter would have been quite solid but on merchant vessels it might have had two or more arched openings or might have been no more than small panels out at the ship's side. The bulkhead details here depended largely on the size of the ship and the locations of various deck fittings. The extent of the quarter or poop deck was determined by the amount of shelter required beneath it.

It will be noted that Raleigh mentioned men, mariners, and the master who must be considered in their seventeenth-century sense when discussing the uses to which the various sections of a ship were put. Presumably Raleigh was writing about the larger armed ships rather than common merchant vessels and by the term 'men' meant the fighting personnel in contrast to the 'mariners' who operated the ships. The captain of a large ship was the military commander and he usually lived in the great cabin. The master of such a ship, subordinate to the captain, was responsible for handling her; it was for him that Raleigh would provide 'one low cabin'. On small merchant vessels the duties of the military captain and the sailing master probably were combined in one person who occupied the great cabin, leaving the small cabin aloft for the mate. Mates and petty officers often slept in cupboard bunks built along a ship's side in enclosed spaces.

Early explorers of the New World found the natives using the hammock for sleeping and this useful article was introduced in ships of the Royal Navy in 1597; they were called at first 'hanging cabbons or beddes'. Their use was not immediately widespread and for many years, particularly in home waters, seamen had only the comfort of a spare sail, a coil of rope, or the bare deck.

There is little doubt that the average medium size merchant ship in which the majority of the North American colonists crossed the Atlantic had two decks in the main hull. These did not necessarily run continuously from bow to stern as became the general practice in warships. The seventeenth-century shipbuilder set his deck levels to suit the space requirements for cargo, crew, and stores; stepped decks in merchant vessels were common through the eighteenth century. A typical arrangement of decks and superstructures for an early seventeenth-century ship is shown in Fig 6.

Considering again for a moment the three methods of presenting the characteristics of a by-gone ship type it is apparent that, in general, neither the artist nor the average model builder has to worry too much about the structure of the vessels they depict. The built-up model is, of

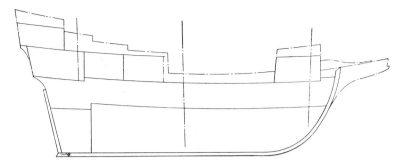

6. *Typical arrangement of decks in an early seventeenth-century ship*

course, a special case as it is created specifically to show a ship's construction. The structure of a vessel has considerable effect on its appearance and on the location of many of the fittings; structure may be adjusted to suit conditions but not ignored as so often seems the case. Neither does the artist nor the model builder have to worry how various pieces of equipment might have been constructed as long as the appearance seems right. Many do not stop to wonder whether seamen could have lived in or worked the vessels that they show.

For a full-size reproduction of an old ship type all these things do have to be considered, some of them in light of the availability of materials. For example, the present day cost of duplicating some of the timber sizes used in earlier ships would be almost prohibitive. Further, such a reproduction would be primarily a museum piece hence problems connected with showing a considerable number of visitors per day through it would require study as they would have an effect on the final arrangement of the vessel.

During a century or so from about 1550 to 1650 there seems to have been considerable change in the methods of framing a ship. There were several reasons for this change including the strength requirements occasioned by the increasing size of ships and weight of armament, better protection against gunfire, and the growing difficulties in the procurement of timber of the proper shapes and sizes. Small boats, from the structural point of view, were generally miniature reproductions of large ships having all framing hewn and sawn to shape. The steam bending of frames was unknown but green planks were often scorched or heated in wet sand to render them pliable enough to be bent around the customary bluff bows of seventeenth-century vessels.

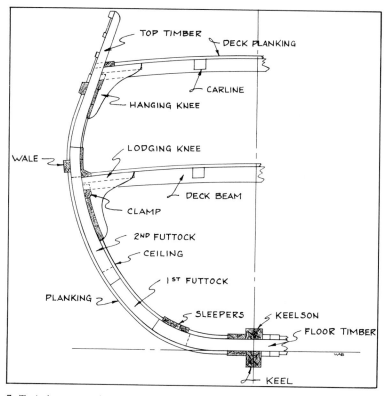

7. Typical structure of a seventeenth-century ship

The structure of typical English vessels during the seventeenth century can best be described in conjunction with Fig 7. The keel was the backbone of the ship on which the entire structure was erected; the need for a ship to be built like a girder with strength in the decks as the upper flange was not known. Across the keel were placed the first pieces of the framing, the floor timbers, roughly square in section and spaced a little over their width apart. The next pieces of framing, the first 'foot-hooks', later corrupted to the present word 'futtocks', were placed between the ends of the floors overlapping from say two to four feet depending on the size of the frames. This overlapping is the old meaning of the word 'scarf' but the term then also meant a carefully fitted joint as at present. Piece by piece the framing was continued until the top of the rails was reached, each successive piece being narrower and thinner than the preceding one. The final pieces of framing were called the top timbers. In a small vessel there might have been only one futtock and a long top timber on each side while in a large ship there were as many as four futtocks and the top timber.

Usually there was no connection between the various futtocks; the whole framing fabric was held together by the binding action of the regular planking on the outside and the ceiling (the old 'sealing' was a better word) on the inside. The futtocks and top timbers composing one or two frames may have been fastened together and erected as a whole to serve as guides but, in general, a ship was put together much as a basket is made, futtocks being added as the planking and ceiling were carried along. There is evidence that wedges called 'glots' were driven alongside the heel of each futtock to force it tightly against the next. Apparently every third or fourth frame was drawn out with a pair of compasses as described earlier and measurements for the intermediate frames taken from the ship. By the end of the seventeenth century it probably was the practice to erect such frames as a whole.

The framing of an actual ship was very irregular, far from the perfection shown by the built-up Admiralty-type models. While it is generally agreed that such models show the form and general appearance of the vessels they represent it is obvious that their construction was standardized. Each frame consists of a floor timber and one futtock and a top timber on each side, all of the same thickness, but it is known as mentioned above, that some vessels had as many as four futtocks of differing thicknesses. It has been suggested that the Admiralty-type models represent the way all ships were built around 1600 when timber supplies were plentiful and the way small vessels continued to be built as long as suitable timber was available. Once a modelmaking convention was established the model builders saw no need to complicate their problems by introducing a larger number of smaller pieces. This conventional method of building models was carried well into the eighteenth century, long after there had been major changes in the actual construction of large ships.[8]

Turning back to ship framing, to help strengthen the important scarf between the floor timbers and the first futtocks, three or four strakes of the ceiling were made extra thick; these were known as the 'sleepers'. To bind the framing on the outside and to add some longitudinal strength to a ship there were several heavy fore-and-aft timbers called 'wales'. These are prominent on all vessels of the period as they also served for decoration, setting off the apparent sheer of the hull in contrast to the deck levels indicated by the gunports. Up to about 1650 shipwrights were careful not to cut the wales for gunports; if there was a conflict either the deck or the wale was stepped. The ends of the widely spaced deck beams rested on longitudinal members on the inside of the frames; these were usually called 'clamps' for the lowest deck and 'risings' for all the others. The beams were secured to the frames at each end by one hanging knee, and one horizontal or 'lodging' knee. Between the main deck beams the deck planking was supported by fore-and-aft 'carlines' and transverse members called 'ledges'.

While beech was sometimes employed for keels practically all of the structure described so far, in English ships at least, was of oak. Deck planking was usually of Scottish or Norwegian pine. Apart from decay the greatest problem of seventeenth-century shipbuilders was that of proper fastenings; these two problems still plague the builders of wooden ships. While it still is common practice to secure outer planking over 1½in in thickness with well-seasoned wooden pegs or 'treenails' (usually pronounced as if spelled 'trunnels'), in the early seventeenth century they were used for such important connections as the securing of the floor timbers to the keel and even for the fastening down of the deck planking. Iron nails then were reserved for securing the light planking of the superstructures and the deck planking to the carlines and ledges. As the century progressed the increased use of iron and other metals for bolts and spikes gave better connections that led to such innovations as the cutting of wales in the way of gunports.

Small open boats were constructed in much the same manner as today. The stem and sternpost were first shaped and erected on the keel. Then four or five full molds fabricated to the correct shape were set at the proper locations on the keel. Light ribbands were sprung around these molds from stem to stern and all measurements for the sawn frames taken from them. Each frame was generally constructed with a floor timber and but one futtock on each side. For boats having carvel or smooth planking the frames were normally set up and then the planking fitted. Clinker-built boats had the planks riveted together before the frames were inserted.

With this necessarily limited background on naval architecture let us turn to one of the better known ships that carried English colonists to North America.

CHAPTER 2

Early Colonists –
The Mayflower

A. INTRODUCTION

At five o'clock in the afternoon of Saturday 20 April 1957, a small steam tug picked up the tow line of a strange little sailing ship lying behind Drake's Island in the sound off Plymouth, England, and started moving toward the open sea. Outside the breakwater, shortly after six o'clock, the tow line was cast off and, one by one, six sails were set on the little ship to catch a light breeze from the west. Thus began a passage that captured the imagination of thousands of people in all parts of the world. The little ship was *Mayflower II*, a reproduction of a typical merchant vessel of the size and type of the *Mayflower* that carried the Pilgrims to North America in 1620. The fifty-four day Atlantic passage of the little ship to Plymouth, Massachusetts, under the command of Captain Alan Villiers is now history.

The departure of *Mayflower II* from Plymouth, England, marked the end of one phase of a combination fairy tale and detective story, the finish of six years of spare time researching, drawing, and calculating. My part in the project started in the spring of 1951 when I was asked by the Governors of Plimoth Plantation, Incorporated, of Plymouth, Massachusetts, to prepare plans and specifications for a *Mayflower*. The Plantation, a non-profit educational foundation organized in 1947 to dramatize the Pilgrim story for modern Americans, had as its ultimate goal a reconstruction of the entire Pilgrim village and its projected program included a representation of the *Mayflower*.

In the spring of 1955 an English group that since the end of World War II had been thinking of building and sailing a *Mayflower* across the Atlantic to further the cause of Anglo-American relations heard of the plans and specifications being prepared for Plimoth Plantation and suggested a sort of merger. In return for use of the plans the English group, under the name of Project Mayflower Limited, proposed to present the ship to the American people with Plimoth Plantation Inc as the permanent custodian. Preliminary arrangements were made, my plans and specifications were sent to England, and the keel of the new *Mayflower* was laid on 28 July 1955 in the yard of J W & A Upham, Brixham, Devon. She was launched on 22 September 1956 and was under sail for the first time on 16 April 1957.

It is difficult to believe that in the mid-twentieth century there would be any group seriously interested in re-creating a full-size early seventeenth-century ship. That there should be two such groups with the same ship in mind is almost inconceivable; this is the fairy tale part of the project. The detective story part concerns the research into the history of the original *Mayflower*; the form, construction and rigging of ships of her period and a multitude of associated problems.

IV. *The keel and floor timbers of* Mayflower II, *November 1955.* (Author)

B. HISTORY

Opinions vary as to which ship is the most important in the maritime history of the United States but the Pilgrims' *Mayflower* stands high on the list. The telling of the Pilgrims' story every year in connection with Thanksgiving Day, the countless pictures and models labelled *Mayflower*, and the usual listings in the catalogues of large libraries might easily lead one to assume that everything is known about the original ship. Actually, the only reliable information concerns the Atlantic crossing and even that is exceedingly scant.

The standard authority on the Pilgrims' crossing to the New World is Governor William Bradford's journal *Of Plimoth Plantation* which he started writing about ten years after their arrival.[1] As might be expected from the time of writing he gave very few definite details about the ship. Now considered a great symbol the *Mayflower* meant so little to Bradford and other early chroniclers of the colony named Plymouth that they neglected to mention her name. For the seamen involved it was only another in a long series of fishing and trading voyages, not worthy of special note. It was not until 1623 that a reference was made in the colony's records to those 'which came first over in the May-Flower' and thus her name is known.

Diligent research, however, has produced some interesting items concerning the original *Mayflower*. This research has been difficult because *Mayflower* was a common name for ships of the period. About twenty vessels bearing that name have been traced but so many researchers have worked on the problem it is unlikely that any new pertinent material will be found. Any modern re-creation of the ship owes much to the work of these people. Variations between the 1957 *Mayflower* and other versions are the result of different interpretations of the available data but none can claim to be more than a representation of a typical merchant ship of the size and type of the Pilgrims' vessel.

Because of leaky topsides and the cracking of a beam during a storm it is generally assumed that the *Mayflower* was an old vessel when she made her now famous voyage in 1620–21. Many sources refer to the ship's master as a Mr Jones and he was long identified as a Thomas Jones who had a rather unsavory reputation. On the basis of Admiralty Court and other records, however, most researchers now accept the conclusion that Thomas Jones could not have been but one Christopher Jones must have been the master of the *Mayflower*. Through the records of the port of London it has been possible to trace

V. *The port bow of* Mayflower II *in April 1956.* (Author)

some of the movements of a *Mayflower* with a Christopher Jones, master, from August 1609 to October 1621.[2] By assuming a neighborly relationship of shipmasters it is possible to trace this *Mayflower* back to 1606. A similar relationship too lengthy to review here is the basis for the remote possibility that she was one of the two *Mayflowers* of London that fought against the Spanish Armada in 1588.[3]

In the port of London records there is an appropriate gap that would allow for the *Mayflower*'s voyage to New England in 1620–21. A passage in Mourt's *Relation. . .* indicates that Captain Jones was familiar with whaling and the voyage records are such that the *Mayflower* could have gone whaling off Greenland but no definite proof of this has been found.[4] The voyages noted below are typical and indicate that she was employed as a normal cargo vessel of the period:

August 1609
To Drontheim, Norway, with hats, hemp, Spanish salt, hops, vinegar, and Gascon wine. From Drontheim – tar, deals, and herring.
May 1612
To Rochelle, France, with cloth of various kinds, stockings, iron stubs, pewter, and virginals.
May 1614
From Hamburg – taffeta, satins, sarsenets, and lawns.
January 1615
From Rochelle – Gascon and Cognac wines.

The unloading of a cargo of salt from Rochelle on 31 October 1621 is the last record of the Christopher Jones *Mayflower* in the London Port Books; the last record of her master is in the register of St Mary's, Rotherhithe, for 1621–22: 'Christopher Jones, buried 5 March'. He left no will on record and his widow was granted a commission of administration. Acting on a petition by Mrs Jones and two of three other part owners of the ship dated 26 May 1624, which described her as 'in ruinis', the High Court of Admiralty appointed four surveyors who valued the *Mayflower* at £128-8s-4d. The term 'in ruinis' has been variously translated to mean actually in ruins, dismantled, or just laid up. The ship's ultimate fate is unknown although claims have been made that a barn in Buckinghamshire was constructed from her timbers and that her masts served as pillars in the Independent Chapel at Abingdon in Berkshire. Neither of these claims have been proved to the satisfaction of competent researchers.[5]

Any attempt to produce a representation of the *Mayflower* – drawing, painting, model, or full-size sailing ship – must start with some estimate of her size but the only information available concerns her tonnage. Governor Bradford mentioned a burden of about nine score tons. One of Captain John Smith's books noted a burden of 160, the papers of the Earl of Southampton recorded 140 tons, while one researcher has used 120 tons. Considering that the *Mayflower* landed 102 passengers and had a crew of perhaps 25 to 30 men, most researchers have accepted Governor Bradford's figure. While many have marvelled that a ship of only 180 tons could have carried so many people, records of similar passages in the early seventeenth century indicate that she was not unduly crowded. One vessel of 150 tons carried 85 passengers and a 350-ton ship had 230 passengers.

As for the probable appearance of the *Mayflower* little agreement was found among marine archaeologists, artists, and authors. A survey of the many prints, paintings, models, and what-have-you purporting to be of this vessel revealed some startling representations; one etching had the square sails set on the after sides of the masts. Governor Bradford was of little help but we can deduce from his journal that the ship had at least one topsail. When he noted that John Howland fell overboard he wrote, '. . . he caught hould of ye top-saile halliards, which hunge overboard. . .'.[6]

The following is a footnote in the Massachusetts Historical Society's edition of Bradford:[7]

> No description or representation of the *Mayflower* other than the brief references in Bradford exists. There is, however, no reason for believing that she differed materially from the merchant vessels of that day or that an English vessel of her class differed materially from a merchant vessel of any other commercial people of Europe. The map-makers of that period almost invariably drew upon some part of their plate one or more vessels, usually the trading types with sails set, and threading their way among the monsters of the deep, often much larger than themselves. Whether the map was English, Dutch, or German, the vessels have the same general appearance.

Considering the size of a sketch that would normally appear on a map the above note is generally true, but there were certain national characteristics that were dictated by the conditions of the coasts and harbors of the various countries. As examples, English harbors allowed the use of deep narrow ships while the shallow waters off the Low Countries led to the development of bluff beamy vessels that drew relatively little water. Details of decoration and fittings varied considerably but printed and manuscript sources indicate a substantial exchange of shipbuilding knowledge. If a ship was damaged at sea the necessary repairs undoubtedly would have been made in the manner standard at the next port visited. A vessel then could have been equipped with items from several countries which leads to the conclusion that when definite details are not available from one country those of another can be adapted. This is particularly true in the cases of countries having extensive mutual commerce.

While there is some technical material concerning the design and construction of late sixteenth- and early seventeenth-century ships, much of our knowledge of such ships comes from old engravings, etchings and paintings. Such knowledge has always been considered somewhat dubious, for it is the result of two interpretations, the artist's interpretation of the ship and our interpretation of his efforts. Some representations seem quite reasonable, others the products of the weirdest possible nightmares. All must be considered on a general basis as there are few named ship portraits of the period. Since the new *Mayflower* has been afloat and under sail, however, opinions as to the credibility of the efforts of some early artists must be revised, for their works compare favorably with photographs of her under sail.

C. DIMENSIONS AND LINES

Following the majority of *Mayflower* researchers I accepted Governor Bradford's burden of about nine score tons for the ship and turned to a study of ship proportions. Ships of the Elizabethan period are commonly thought to have been quite tubby in shape. This is a fallacy that arose from the practice of comparing tables of dimensions giving the keel lengths of these ships with the gundeck lengths commonly given for later vessels. A better comparison may be obtained by adding to the keel length the forward rake of the stem and the aft rake of the sternpost; the sum of these two was usually equal to the maximum breadth. The hulls of naval vessels of a century later actually were fuller as increases in armament required more displacement in the ends to keep the flexible wooden hulls from drooping out of shape.

William Borough, comptroller of the English Navy from 1589 to 1598, listed the following proportions for vessels of his time:[8]

1. The shortest, broadest and deepest order – To have the length by the keel double the breadth amidships and the depth in hold half that breadth. This order is used in some merchant ships for most profit.
2. The mean and best proportion for shipping for merchandise like-

wise very serviceable for all purposes. Length of keel two or two and a quarter that of beam. Depth of hold eleven-twenty-fourths that of beam.

3. The largest order for galleons or ships for the wars made for the most advantage of sailing. Length of keel three times the beam. Depth of hold two-fifths of beam.

Considering these proportions and those of a number of known merchant vessels of the period the *Mayflower* might have had a keel length ranging from 52.4ft to 73.0ft, a breadth from 24.3ft to 27.0ft, and a depth of 10.1ft to 13.1ft. The reader may make his own choice but the combination must be such that

$$K \times B \times \frac{D}{100} \text{ equals about 180.}$$

For the re-creation of the *Mayflower* the original concept of the Governors of Plimoth Plantation was to follow in general one of the several existing model designs but they realized that many details would have to be changed. The logical one to use was that on display in Pilgrim Hall, Plymouth, Massachusetts, which was designed by and constructed under the supervision of Dr R C Anderson. This model, described by Dr Anderson in the July 1926 issue of *The Mariner's Mirror* (vol 12, no 3), had a keel length of 64ft, a breadth of 26ft, and a depth of 11ft. At the time I believed that the available data indicated a slightly shorter and narrower but deeper ship. The proportions of Dr Anderson's model, however, were well within the possible range and I drew a set of preliminary plans using his dimensions and basic features.

In the spring of 1952 my wife and I took a long combination research and vacation trip to visit the important marine museums in London, Stockholm, Elsinore, Amsterdam and Paris as well as some smaller collections. Prints of the preliminary plans were discussed with competent authorities on old ships in the various museums. In general the preliminary work was acceptable but there were many suggestions about details that would require more or less extensive changes. After returning home and considering all my notes it seemed best to scrap all the preliminary work and to start anew. In short, as it was likely that I would be criticized for making changes in adapting any model design to a full-size ship it would be better to present an entirely new design that could be judged on its own merits. This I did.

THE MAYFLOWER

If the *Mayflower*, Christopher Jones, master, of the London Port Books be accepted as the Pilgrims' ship *Mayflower*, she was known to have been afloat in 1609. A few reasonable assumptions push the date back to February 1606. If she was new at about that time her probable trade and builder would have to be considered in selecting her proportions; if old, perhaps one of the anti-Armada fleet, there was no way of knowing how far back proportions should be investigated. The further back one goes the more meager becomes the suitable information. A common merchant ship intended for the cloth, timber and wine trades, in all of which the Christopher Jones *Mayflower* was employed from time to time, would have required as much stowage space as possible. This pointed toward a short length and relatively large breadth and depth for a given tonnage as the structure of such a ship occupies a smaller percentage of the internal volume compared with a longer, narrower and shallower vessel.

Changes in the appearance and proportions of ships are usually noted first in the larger, more important vessels. In recent years these have been the large passenger liners; in the early seventeenth century they would have been the royal ships and those of a few favored merchants. An ordinary merchant probably would have sought a shipwright operating a small yard who had been building to conservative proportions that had proved successful over a period of years. Even so, any shipwright seeing the great new royal ships would have been influenced somewhat by them. Assuming the *Mayflower* to have been built in the very early years of the seventeenth century, prior to 1606, a general increase in the length/breadth ratio of the royal ships might have led this shipwright to improve somewhat on Borough's ratios of 2 to 2.25 for merchant ships.

Included in the study of proportions was the small naval vessel *Crane* built in 1590 by Richard Chapman. Her dimensions – keel length 60ft, breadth 26ft, and depth 13ft – were duplicated in an example in Mathew Baker's notebook, mentioned earlier, which indicates that at least two shipwrights of the period were thinking along the same lines. Both held Letters Patent as master shipwrights building royal ships; probably their choices of proportions would have been used by common builders within a decade. The *Crane*'s proportions – length/breadth ratio of 2.31 with the depth equal to half the breadth – indicated a conservative design of good capacity yet an improvement on Borough's merchant vessels. They were chosen for the new *Mayflower* whose principal dimensions worked out as follows: keel length 58ft, breadth 25ft, and depth 12.5ft. By the tonnage rule mentioned earlier these gave a burden of 181, close enough to Governor Bradford's 'about nine score' that odd inches were not considered.

With the dimensions finally settled there came the actual process of drawing the lines plan which followed the routine outlined in Chapter 1. The midship section shown in Fig 3 is actually that of the new *May-flower*. Mathew Baker's method of locating its proper position with respect to the forward end of the keel, shown in Fig 8, was carried out as follows:

Length of keel = ab = 58ft 0in
58ft 0in ÷ 3 = 19ft 4in = db
ac = cb = 29ft 0in
cb − db = 29ft 0in − 19ft 4in = 9ft 8in = cd
cd ÷ 3 = 9ft 8in ÷ 3 = 3ft 2⅔in
cd ÷ 2 = 9ft 8in ÷ 2 = 4ft 10in
ag = 29ft 0in + 3ft 2⅔in + 4ft 10in = 37ft 0⅔in
gb = 58ft 0in − 37ft 0⅔in = 20ft 11⅓in

For the new ship the actual location used was 20ft 11in abaft the forward end of the keel. By a 'ruell of proportion' for calculating trim this midship section location would give the ship a 23in trim by the stern and so it proved when she was launched. For the profile of the ship the rake aft of the sternpost was set at 4ft thus the forward rake of the stem, assuming that the sum of the two equalled the breadth, was 21ft. The stem might have been drawn as a single arc or a combination of two arcs with the lower having the shorter radius; the latter was chosen in this case.

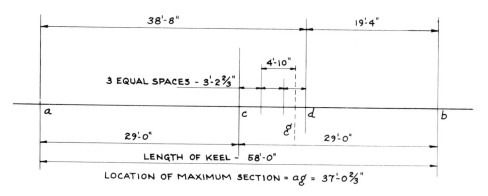

8. *Plot showing location of maximum section on keel*

VI. Mayflower II, *framing from astern, April 1956.* (Author)

With the midsection drawn, its location on the keel calculated, and the profile set down the next step was to draw the narrowing and rising lines for the floor and maximum breadth. The half breadth of the floor was taken from the midsection and tapered to zero at the ends by arcs of circles. The floor rising line was also composed of two arcs which intersected the stem at 5ft 3in and the sternpost at 7ft above the top of the keel.

THE MAYFLOWER

As shown in Fig 4 long radius arcs shape the side from the stern to about the forward end of the keel with a short radius arc at the bow. By use of a diagram in the Baker MS the after part may be made somewhat wider than a true arc. This diagram has been cited as the basis for dating this MS as circa 1586, for it bears the note 'The firste that wase mad by this the Vanguard'. She was a large ship of 449 tons burden built by Mathew Baker at Woolwich in 1586. On the premise that the new ship should represent a burdensome carrier the bluffest of the bow lines shown in the MS and the above mentioned diagram were used in drawing her breadth narrowing line. In the absence of any definite instructions about the height of breadth line it was proportioned from a drawing in the MS.

Using these narrowing and rising lines the sections forward and aft were drawn by progressively changing the positions of the centers of the three arcs or 'sweeps' used in delineating the midship section. The radius of the floor sweep was proportionately shortened at each successive section until it was zero at the stem and sternpost. Two problems remained, the reverse curve from the floor sweep down to the keel and the shape of the topsides. By using instructions from a manuscript of about 1670 and doing a bit of trial-and-error work reasonable looking reverses were drawn. For the topsides, the sections aft were all straight lines of decreasing slope from the midsection to the stern. Forward, the slope of the midsection was worked into a reverse curve so that the forecastle rail was nearly vertical.

The new ship's lines so drawn were believed to be as typical of the period as reasonable study and effort could produce but, as with any such project, further research uncovered more information. In 1955, too late to change the plan, an anonymous and undated treatise on shipbuilding of about 1620 was obtained from the Admiralty Library; as mentioned in Chapter 1 this was published by the Society for Nautical Research in 1958. The fact that the floor sweep radius did not reduce to zero at the ends but, in effect, crossed the centerline and that at the ends the floor sweep was not part of the section but served only to guide the bottom of the body sweep would have affected the lines as drawn only below the six foot waterline. The net changes would have been small.

Considering the methods employed in drawing the lines they were surprisingly good and it was believed that the ship would be reasonably fast under sail. The return trip of the original *Mayflower* to England in thirty-one days proved that she was no slouch. The poor windward sailing ability of ships of the period can be attributed more to the sails and rigging than to hull form. The maximum speed of a bit over eight knots attained by the new ship, not as high as expected, probably was limited by the dragging transom as mentioned in the first chapter. On the other hand she moves easily in a light breeze. Had modern methods been used in drawing the lines some sharp curves would have been smoothed out but many of the characteristics of early seventeenth-century ships would have been lost.

D. ARRANGEMENT AND CONSTRUCTION

The typical arrangement of decks shown in Fig 6 is actually that of the new *Mayflower*. It follows the evidence of old paintings, prints, and plans as well as the recommendation of Sir Walter Raleigh.

A problem peculiar to the arrangement and construction of a ship reproduction that must accommodate a large number of visitors is that of deck heights. In some locations small vessels of the Elizabethan period had relatively low deck heights but clearances between decks became greater as ship size increased. Scale drawings show that some vessels of about the size of the *Mayflower* had the tops of their upper deck beams about 5ft above those of the lower deck; on large ships the corresponding figure was as much as 9ft. Deducting the thickness of the deck planking under foot and the depth of the beams overhead the clear dimensions might be only 4ft and 7½ft.

A seaman of the Elizabethan period could be expected to accustom himself to living and scuttling around in a restricted 4ft 'tween deck space but not so with a present day visitor, especially as man's average height has increased noticeably during the past three and a half centuries. In consideration of the heads of modern-sized visitors the greatest dimension that could be justified – 7ft molded, ie from top of beam to top of beam – was chosen for most of the deck heights in the new *Mayflower* which gave about 6ft clear under the beams. The 7ft dimension was taken from a scale profile of a vessel of about her size in the Baker MS (60ft × 24ft × 12ft). The average visitor can walk through the ship without ducking although most do. Of course, between the beams, spaced about 4ft apart, the clearance is greater. Even with 6ft of clear space and a total complement of but 33, one of the crew of the new ship has written of 'the lack of space and elementary sanitation, the ghastly authenticity of Mayflower'.[9] The small master's cabin is even more cramped as it has a molded deck height of 6ft with about 9in less in the clear under the beams.[10]

Most of the structural midsections in the Baker MS show the lower deck at side slightly below the height of maximum breadth, the

THE MAYFLOWER

position varying from 11.7 to 16 percent of the depth. A few have the deck at the maximum breadth and this was the practice in later years. On the midsection of the new *Mayflower* the lower deck was located at 11ft above the top of the keel or 12 percent of the depth below the maximum breadth.

Two items had to be considered in fixing the positions of the lower deck at the ends. Forward, the hawse holes for the anchor cables had to be under the beakhead but above the lower deck. Aft, ports in the stern for guns on the lower deck had to be under the main transom beam at the head of the sternpost. A line connecting three points with the foregoing considerations in mind might be straight or even have a reverse curve similar to the popular sheer line for modern yachts. The available evidence shows, however, the early seventeenth-century ship-wrights used a normal sheer line – low in the middle and high at the ends – but such a line often required steps in the deck toward the ends to locate properly the hawse pipes and stern ports. Such steps were usually down hence termed falls but there are examples of rises. In the smaller vessels the forward step often was not needed and this was the situation in the new ship. With the lower deck located the other decks were run in at the pre-determined deck heights.

Turning briefly to the construction of the new ship, because of timber supplies and strength requirements it was decided quite early that her framing would not follow early seventeenth-century practice but would be of the modern double sawn-futtock type. Each frame is fabricated of a number of short overlapping sections each of half the thickness of the full frame. 'Modern' as applied to this type of framing is relative only; while used today for heavy construction it can be traced back to about 1700. Fig 7 is actually a structural section of the new ship as she would have been built in the seventeenth century.

The basic scantlings for the new *Mayflower* were derived from scale drawings in the Baker MS, old specifications, and late seventeenth-century scantling tables. As it was expected that she would be built in the United States standard structural lumber sizes available there were specified where possible. The sizes and arrangement of some structural members were chosen, however, for reasons other than historical accuracy, the future use of the vessel being a prime consideration.

The Governors of Plimoth Plantation authorized the preparation of the plans and specifications that led eventually to the building of the new *Mayflower* on the basis of a ship to float but not necessarily to sail. As work progressed Plantation records indicated a possible 5000 visitors per day at the height of the tourist season and the two hurricanes Carol and Edna of 1954 demonstrated what could happen again leading to the concept of a dry-land ship built on a concrete foundation from the waterline up. In the eyes of public safety officials such a structure would not be a ship but a place of public assembly subject to certain regulations concerning strength. This consideration determined the structure of the several decks which, though patterned after early seventeenth-century practice, were made considerably heavier. Although deck weights are high in the hull and adversely affect the stability of a floating hull, no changes were made when construction was started in England as the ship would still be subjected to crowd loads when in her final exhibition berth.

The spacing of the beams for the lower and upper decks was set at 4ft; those for the superstructure decks were spaced to suit local conditions. Fig 7 shows the ends of the beams supported by fore-and-aft clamps, the upper member of which is notched. The clamps of the main decks are composed of several pieces as it would have been impractical to specify anything like the 18in width called for in a 1583 Dutch contract. To economize on material when the ship was built the hanging knees of the lower deck were placed under the beam ends in modern fashion but those for the higher decks are lapped on the sides of the beams in the proper seventeenth-century manner.

The beakhead deserves some comment at this point; it is admittedly of an old type in keeping with the design premise, a conservative type of ship built about 1600 by a shipwright operating a small yard. The beakheads of many models seem to have been stuck on the bow as an afterthought; from some viewing points almost any beakhead will give that impression. Careful study showed, however, that in profile most of the old beakheads made structural sense by having some of their rails landing on the main hull wales and moldings. This was particularly true for vessels shown in the Baker MS after which the beakhead of the new *Mayflower* was patterned.

By this time (1975) some readers of this book may have visited the new *Mayflower* hence are familiar with her arrangement but for those who have not a quick tour is in order. Omitting the process of getting on board and staying out of the hold which can be assumed full of bales, chests, crates, and barrels – but little or no furniture – the tour can start on the lower deck at the very bow. Here is the manger, a wooden bin under the hawse holes to collect water that might slop in through them; at sea the hawse holes would be plugged. Looking aft we get the impression of a 6ft high tunnel stretching 78ft back to the transom. Here, too, is the foremast with the bowsprit on its starboard

VII. *Ready for launching, September 1956.* (Author)

side coming in through the upper deck and secured to the lower deck. Just abaft the foremast are the heavy riding bitts, port and starboard, that support a heavy horizontal windlass barrel; a single pawl bitt stands on the centerline. A few researchers have suggested that the windlass should have been on the upper deck abaft the forecastle;

perhaps they are right but that location would have created problems with cable leads and boat stowage. To starboard near the foremast is a companion ladder with a hatch over in the upper deck. The anchor cables are normally stowed in the hold being passed down through a small hatch abaft the windlass.

The mainmast is slightly abaft the mid-length of the lower deck and just forward of it is the main cargo hatch. Thus from the windlass to the mainmast there is a fairly clear space about 26ft long and 22ft wide obstructed only by a few light pillars. On normal trading voyages non-perishable cargo probably was carried here. Abreast the mainmast, port and starboard, are the log pumps which discharge on the upper deck. In the seventeenth century the pumps might have discharged on the watertight lower deck with the water flowing overboard through leather-flapped scuppers along the sides. The manger is fitted with similar scuppers. Chain pumps were invented during the reign of the first Queen Elizabeth but probably were used then only in the larger more important ships.

About 10ft abaft the mainmast is the double capstan that extends above the upper deck where bars may be fitted, too, enabling from 8 to 16 men to heave at one time. Anchors can be weighed faster with the capstan than with the windlass but a surge of the ship is liable to throw the men from the bars. In merchant ships the capstan served mainly for hoisting the yards and topmasts and for any special lifts including cargo. Above the gunports in the transom are two small holes, 'cat-holes', through which hawsers may be led to the capstan when it is necessary to haul the ship astern.

Below the fall of the lower deck, about 12ft forward of the transom, is a bulkhead in the hold and the small compartment thus formed would have served as the powder magazine. A small hatch gives access to it. The after part of the main hold is used for ship's stores and there is a stores hatch just forward of the fall.

In this 'tween deck space there are ten gunports, two in the stern and four in each side. The original ship may have carried two guns for her stern ports but in view of the scarcity of ordnance and the crowded conditions with the Pilgrims on board she may have had only two on each side. Ordnance types of the early seventeenth century had fanciful names and there was considerable variation between pieces of the same type. The largest gun in general use on shipboard was the demi-cannon, a piece about 10ft long of 6½in caliber weighing about 6000lbs. In ordinary merchant ships smaller pieces, minions of 3¼in caliber and falcons of 2in, were used as carriage guns with perhaps a few small swivels on the rails.

Coming in through a centerline port over the main transom beam is the 15ft long tiller whose forward end is supported by a light transverse beam. Passing through a roller fitted in the upper deck is a vertical wooden staff, the whipstaff, whose lower end has an iron ring that slips over the forward end of the tiller. Going up a ladder through the upper deck stores hatch we enter the steerage where the helmsman works the whipstaff which can move the rudder about ten degrees to either side. Just forward of the whipstaff is the binnacle, a small wooden cabinet that holds the compass, candles to light it, the traverse board, and the sand glasses that measure the time. The traverse board, which resembles a circular cribbage board, was used to mark the length of time sailed on a particular compass course and estimates of speed during each watch.

Through a small hatch in the halfdeck the helmsman can by day see the sails on the mainmast to aid in steering and at all times receive orders from the officer on deck who is conning the ship. It is worth noting that while the left side of the ship was the 'larboard' side when referring to anything located there, the order to the helmsman even in 1620 was 'Port the helm'. And with the whipstaff method of steering the top of the staff, the rudder, and the ship's head go in the same direction just as with the approved modern method of arranging the steering gear.

As applied in ships of the period the term 'cabin' is a bit confusing. In some cases it meant what it does today, a room or compartment in a ship, but it also meant a temporary shelter set up by the ship's carpenter. A third definition was some sort of a hanging contraption that could be folded up to the deck above; this might even have been a simple hammock. Still another type was a berth with a hinged or sliding door much like the cupboard type bunks that may still be seen in old Dutch cottages. Berths or 'cabins' of this latter type would normally be found in the steerage but were omitted from the new ship to leave walking space for visitors.

We enter the great cabin at the stern through a door to starboard; there is a small fall in the upper deck here to make this cabin as spacious as possible. The mizzenmast is stepped just abaft the bulkhead. When the Pilgrims were on board this cabin probably was cluttered with a number of temporary bunks but the normal fittings would have been quite simple. Across the after end under the three diamond-paned windows is a built-in settee with a bolted-down table in front of it. Other furniture would have been a berth with drawers under on the port side forward; a cabinet for storing books, charts, navigating instruments, mugs, dishes, and table cutlery; a long bench; and one or two three-legged stools. A couple of lamps or candle lanterns, a musket, a brace of pistols, and a cutlass hanging on the bulkhead would complete the equipment.

Going through a door in the forward steerage bulkhead we find the upper part of the capstan, the mainmast, and the log pumps. Just abaft the mast and slightly to starboard is a 12in square vertical timber extending 4ft above the deck and fitted with four large sheaves; its base is secured to a lower deck beam. This is the main knight which serves as the lower block of the main halyard. Similar knights are fitted abaft the foremast on this deck and just forward of the mizzenmast on the halfdeck. The term 'knight' derives from the fact that on large elaborately-decorated ships the tops of these timbers usually were carved to represent a helmeted knight's head.

Between the mainmast and the forecastle is a long hatch, 'the gratings', which were just what the name implies, a series of wooden gratings supported by strong beams. Their main purpose was to provide light and air to the 'tween deck space. Normal hatches were fitted with sectional wooden covers made watertight by tarpaulins secured with lashings but the gratings were covered with tarpaulins only in very foul weather. The ship's boats usually were stowed on the gratings although in all but the worst weather the long boat was usually towed astern.

Passing into the forecastle through a double door on the centerline we see the upper deck companion hatch to starboard, as noted earlier, and the galley is to port 'especially being contrived in furnaces for the saving of wood in long journeys'. The latter may have applied in large ships but ordinary vessels apparently had no more than a simple hearth fitted with a spit and a kettle crane. The fore knight stands a little abaft the mast to port; there is a small hatch in the forecastle deck for the halyard falls.

Small doors port and starboard in the forward forecastle bulkhead give the crew access to the beakhead. The names of the upper deck bulkheads are slightly confusing as this forward one is the 'beakhead bulkhead', the after forecastle bulkhead is the 'forward cubbridge head', while that under the forward end of the halfdeck is the 'after cubbridge head'. The term 'cubbridge head' comes from medieval days; its derivation is too lengthy to discuss here.

Going aft again we climb up to the halfdeck. As built, there was a short length of portable grating at its forward end to allow the capstan spindle to be hauled out and replaced if broken or badly worn. In consideration for the high heels of lady visitors this was planked over in the mid-1960s. Part of the forward rail here is a small belfry for the ship's bell. At the stern is the master's cabin with its door to starboard and a ladder to the poop deck above on the port wide. Light is provided by small diamond-paned windows, one in each side and one in the bulkhead. The cabin's bulkhead is just far enough abaft the mizzen-mast to allow the lateen mizzen yard to swing between them as it is shifted to the lee side of the mast when the ship is tacked.

Now take this brief description of the new *Mayflower* and add on the weather decks a multitude of cleats, kevels and pins for belaying the running rigging with coils of rope on each. Place on board 102 assorted Pilgrims and colonists plus a crew of 25 or 30. Stow in the hold all the goods needed for founding and maintaining a colony for a considerable period. Clutter up the 'tween deck space with a cut-down shallop. Add cold weather, cold water dripping on all through leaky decks and topsides, and toss liberally around the North Atlantic for two months. Season the situation with the inevitable difficult relations between members of a large group living in confined spaces. When the ship is finally riding safely at anchor off the tip of Cape Cod one cannot help but admire the courage and fortitude of the little band whose condition was described by Governor Bradford:

> But here I cannot but stay and make a pause, and stand half amazed at this poor people's present condition; and so I think will the reader, too, when he well considers the same. Being thus passed the vast ocean . . . they had now no friends to welcome them nor inns to entertain or refresh their weather beaten bodies; no houses or much less towns to repair to, to seek for succour.

E.   MASTING AND RIGGING

The original *Mayflower* may have had one of the two-masted rigs mentioned in the first chapter but as the consensus of researchers favored the standard three-masted rig it was chosen for the new ship. Once this decision was made the immediate problem was to select the sizes of the various spars. There are three good sources for the needed information – Mathew Baker's notebook, the anonymous MS *A Most Excellent Mannor for the Building of Shippes* in the library of the Royal Institution of Naval Architects (hereafter cited as the RINA MS), and Mainwaring's *The Seaman's Dictionary.* None give dimensions for all the spars of a ship but by using all three a reasonable set of dimensions was worked out for the new *Mayflower.*

		Baker MS	RINA MS	Main-waring	New Ship
Spar Dimensions					
Mainmast	l	71−3	67−6	60−0	67−6
	d	21¼		20	20½
Main topmast	l	30−9	33−9	30−0	33−9
	d	9¼		10	9
Foremast	l		57−10¼	48−0	57−9
	d	18¼		16	17
Fore topmast	l	26−3	28−11⅛	24−0	29−0
	d	7¼		8	7½
Mizzenmast	l			30−0	41−8
	d	11¼		10	10½
Bowsprit	l		57−10¼	48−0	57−9
	d	14½		16	13½
Main yard	l	58−6	54−0	48−4	54−0
	d	14¼		12	13½
Main topsail yard	l	19−6		20−8½	21−6
	d	4⅞		5¼	5⅜
Fore yard	l	43−6	40−6	38−8	40−6
	d	11		9⅝	10
Fore topsail yard	l	14−7½		16−7	16−3
	d	3⅝		4⅛	4⅛
Mizzen yard	l		40−6		40−6
	d				10
Spritsail yard	l	32−7½	30−4½		30−4½
	d	8¼			6¼

l = length in feet and inches; d = diameter in inches

Mathew Baker's notebook contains simple charts from which, by laying a straightedge from an index point to a value on a basic scale, lengths and diameters of various spars can be read off intermediate scales. For the lengths of the masts the basic scale is for half the breadth plus half the depth; the chart for mast diameters is based on the length of the mainmast. The basic scale for the lengths of the yards is the keel length minus twice the breadth with the difference divided by nine and added to the breadth. The same chart using as the basic scale the length of the main yard gives the diameters of the various yards.

VIII. *Fitting out* Mayflower II *in dry-dock.* (Popperfoto)

In the RINA MS the length of the mainmast in yards is three-fifths of the sum of the breadth and depth in feet. The foremast and bowsprit are six-sevenths of the mainmast while the topmasts are half their lower masts. The length of the main yard in yards is equal to one-third the sum of half the keel length plus the breadth in feet. The fore and mizzen yards are three-quarters of the main yard while the spritsail yard is three-quarters of the fore yard.

Mainwaring based the length of his mainmast on the ship's breadth, four-fifths of which in feet is the length of the mast in yards. The

46

foremast and bowsprit are four-fifths of the mainmast while the mizzenmast is half its length. Topmasts are half the lengths of their lower masts. All masts have one inch of diameter for each yard of length. The length of the main yard is five-sixths of the keel length. The fore yard is four-fifths of the main yard while the topsail yards are three-sevenths of their lower yards. The lower and topsail yards are three-quarters of an inch and the spritsail and mizzen yards half an inch in diameter for each yard of length. Mainwaring noted that neither the proportions for the masts nor the yards are absolute: '. . . if a man will have his mast short he may the bolder make his topmast long' and '. . . he that will have a taunt mast may have the narrower yards (and so contrary)'.

Based on the dimensions of the new *Mayflower* the table on page 45 gives the spar lengths and diameter according to the three sources as well as those selected for the new ship. In general the lengths are based on the RINA MS with the appropriate diameters read from Baker's charts. The topsail yards are about two-fifths of their lower yards, longer than Baker's one-third but shorter than Mainwaring's three-sevenths.

Fig 9 shows the outboard profile and sail plan of the new *Mayflower*. The detailed information needed for locating the masts and for the various items of rigging came from a contemporary treatise on rigging.[11] Mainwaring's dictionary, the published works of Anderson,[12] Miller,[13] and Moore,[14] and drawings in the Baker MS. Space does not permit a complete treatise on seventeenth-century rigging hence the paragraphs to follow will be limited to a discussion of some of the unusual items and differences between the sail plan and what was fitted on the ship for her Atlantic passage.

First we might note the athwartship ropes supporting the fore- and mainmasts. Today the average sailor would call them 'shrouds' but there is confusion as to what they were called in the seventeenth century. According to rigging data the group included shrouds (4, 5, 6, or 8 per side depending on the burden of the ship), swifters on the mainmast only, and backstays. Depending on the reading of one source swifters were single or double, and all the backstays were single. Four shrouds per side were fitted on both fore- and mainmasts; two swifters plus a backstay gave a total of seven ropes for the mainmast while the single backstay forward made the total five for the foremast.

Judging from pictorial evidence ratlines were fitted across all the above regardless of name. According to Dr Anderson the ratlines were clove hitched to all instead of having seized eye splices at the ends as in

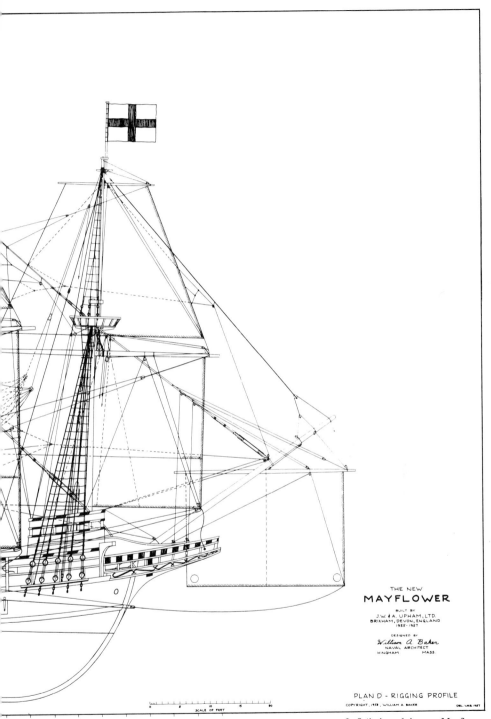

THE NEW
MAYFLOWER

BUILT BY
J.W. & A. UPHAM, LTD.
BRIXHAM, DEVON, ENGLAND
1955-1957

DESIGNED BY
William A. Baker
NAVAL ARCHITECT
HINGHAM   MASS.

PLAN D - RIGGING PROFILE

COPYRIGHT, 1958, WILLIAM A. BAKER   DEL. LAB. 1957

SCALE OF FEET

9. *Sail plan of the new* Mayflower

49

later day practice. This was done on the new ship with the short ends seized down but the ratlines were kept clear of the main backstay which had the main topsail brace and mizzen bowline pulling on it.

The shrouds, swifters and backstays are secured to the hull by the usual system of deadeyes and lanyards. The deadeyes, however, differ from those usually seen today; they have a slight melon-seed shape, flat sides, and are quite thin, somewhat less than twice the thickness of the shroud or stay to which they are fitted. They are based on actual seventeenth-century examples dug from the harbor of Kalmar, Sweden. The lower deadeyes are fastened to the hull by short lengths of chain.

The lower yards are not secured permanently aloft by metal fittings as in later times but can be lowered to the deck. All yards but that for the spritsail are hoisted by ties and halyards. Based on the best evidence the double ties of the lower yards pass through smooth holes cut in the cheeks of the fore- and mainmasts rather than over sheaves that might fail under the strain. The lateen and topsail yards have single ties working through holes in the masts. Normally light purchases called 'jeers' were fitted to supplement the ties and halyards of the lower yards, safety devices that increased in size and power and eventually took over the whole job. As the new *Mayflower* was to make but one major passage and that with new rigging the jeers were not fitted.

Each yard is held close to its respective mast by a parrel, an assemblage of vertical wooden bars known as 'ribs' and heavy wooden rollers called 'trucks', all threaded on and bound together by a rope. Seventeenth-century ships would have had woven rope mats fitted between the lower yards and the masts and perhaps on the other yards as well to prevent galling. Ships of later periods had heavy wooden saddles fitted on the yards to ride on the masts. For convenience leather-lined saddles of oak were fitted on the new *Mayflower* for her Atlantic passage but they have since been removed.

Many of the leads of the lifts and braces controlling the yards seemed strange and temptation to use what became standard in the later days of sail had to be overcome. Items in this category were the various braces that were secured to stays and shrouds, very flexible points of attachment, and the lower yard lift blocks located below the tops.

Generally speaking ships of the Elizabethan period were propelled by the square sails on the fore- and mainmasts; the spritsail under the bowsprit and the lateen mizzen were primarily for balance. The ship was put on her desired course and the latter two sails adjusted so that but little rudder action was needed to keep her there. The topsails were considered light sails and were the first taken in as the wind increased; there were no reef points for reducing their area. The area of the fore and main courses, the mizzen, and sometimes the spritsail could be reduced by unlacing a strip of canvas along the foot called a 'bonnet'. Large ships often had one or two additional strips termed 'drabblers' laced to the bonnets. The new ship has bonnets for her courses and mizzen only; drabblers were not provided.

For handling the sails – setting and furling – there were, in general, all the ropes that became standard on later day square-riggers but, as with the gear for the yards, there were some unusual leads along with a few items that were gradually eliminated from ships with the passing of time. Three buntlines each were specified for the fore and main courses but none for the topsails although sources of information differed on this point. For the Atlantic crossing these were increased to five on the main course, four on the fore, and two on each of the topsails; none could deny that they were not useful.

Perhaps the most complicated bit of gear used in furling each of the courses and the mizzen was the assemblage of pendants and falls called a 'martnet'. It is obvious from some pictorial representations that many marine artists of the period did not understand their use or how they were rigged. The basic purpose of the martnets was to haul the leeches of a sail up to its yard and to form a six-legged net around the sail. In earlier times when it was the practice to lower the yards when furling the fore- and mainsails, which could only be done after the topsails had been taken in, the upper pendants were secured below the tops and the assemblage tightened and did its job as the yard went down. By 1620 topsails often were carried over furled courses and to make the martnets effective the upper pendants were secured to the topmast heads as shown on the rigging profile.

The rigging profile shows the fore, main, spritsail, and mizzen sheets rigged with purchases. While these items and certain other gear seemed quite heavy, the reason may be found in conditions at sea around the time of the original *Mayflower*. A ship's master considered himself lucky if he set sail with a crew twice as large as needed to work his vessel. This was because of the losses he knew would occur from sickness caused by poor food and living conditions and those caused by conflicts with pirates and ships of unfriendly nations. Then with perhaps only a few of the crew able to work, purchases definitely were necessary to handle the sails and other gear. Some of the new *Mayflower*'s crew had served on the *Pequod* during the filming of

THE MAYFLOWER

Melville's *Moby Dick* where it was found that with a modern healthy crew certain purchases were not required. For the same reason the aforementioned sheets were singled up for the new ship's Atlantic passage.

At the time of the new *Mayflower*'s sailing trial no-one on board had set or trimmed a spritsail and it was hard to believe some of the positions shown in old prints. Before the wind there was no doubt but that the yard should be roughly parallel to the water's surface but for windward work it was readily apparent that such a position would not do as there was nothing to hold the leech of the sail taut. Then the yard was trimmed like any other by pulling on the braces with a slight adjustment of the lifts. This put the lee yard arm high in the air, made the yard itself the leading edge similar to a lateen sail – just like the old prints – and there was no more trouble.

If the setting of the spritsail was confusing at first the lateen mizzen seemed even more so, for it was to be shifted to the lee side of the mast on each tack. Because of the mizzen stay, shrouds, and main topsail braces it could not be swung forward of the mast as on the Arabian dhows so it had to be topped to a vertical position and the foot of the yard carried around the after side of the mast. While seemingly difficult this is relatively simple in practice as the mizzen does not have the same taper in each direction but is much heavier at the foot. One man hauling on the lift runner can raise the yard to the vertical while two others ease the foot around the mast, unhooking and rehooking the bowlines as it passes.

Early seventeenth-century ships did not have footropes on the yards for the seamen to stand on when furling the sails. According to pictorial evidence the men sat straddling the yards but it is a bit of a mystery how they managed to gather up a course or a spritsail and pass gaskets around it. The topsail yards, however, were short enough that it was possible to reach almost to the yard arms from the top. Most old pictures show the furled sails hanging rather loosely below the yards; in all probability they were seldom if ever furled in the tighter smooth manner of the smart packet and clipper ships. Common sense as well as modern safety regulations dictated the fitting of footropes on the yards of the new *Mayflower*.

IX. *The standing rigging nears completion early in 1957.* (Popperfoto)

THE MAYFLOWER

A final word about the rope work in general. Rope work is one of the arts of a sailor and the appearance of a sailing ship was judged by the finish of her rigging. It is true even of yachts today although the number of chrome fittings or winches seem to be new standards. The highest development of rope work came during the nineteenth century on packet ships, clipper ships, and particularly on whaling vessels where the men had plenty of time to devote to it. There is little definite information on just how things were done in the early seventeenth century but, in rigging the new *Mayflower*, it seemed reasonable to assume that everything was done in the simplest fashion with no fancy work.

F. BUILDING AND TRIALS

On 28 July 1955 the keel of the new *Mayflower* was officially laid with appropriate ceremonies in a small shipyard in the town of Brixham, Devon, England, not far from the port of Dartmouth where the original *Mayflower* and her consort, the *Speedwell*, sought refuge after the latter sprang a leak at sea. Actually 4 July saw the first section of the keel positioned in the yard of the firm chosen to build the ship, J W and A Upham Ltd, which had been building vessels there since 1838. The firm could trace its existence back to 1807 but it is not known just where on the harbor the earlier vessels were built.

In 1955 the affairs of the company were guided by three directors – Percy A Upham, his son Stuart A, and J H Holman. Both Uphams were natives of Brixham while Mr Holman came from Cornwall which, according to local saying, is just across the river from England. The bulk of the work fell on the shoulders of Mr Stuart, to use yard terminology, but in spite of his eighty-odd years, Mr Percy, who had worked in the yard since boyhood, was there every day to check on the work. The fact that the *Mayflower* put to sea and successfully completed a trans-Atlantic passage with but two hours' trial spoke volumes for the loving care that the entire personnel of the Upham yard devoted to the ship.

In spite of the fact that the keel was laid in July visitors to the yard saw little apparent progress until November because of two big jobs that had to be done. The first was the 'lofting' of the lines, the process of transferring the dimensions of each frame of the ship from the plan to full size in chalk on a shed floor. From the full size body plan molds were made of thin wood which were used in cutting out the futtocks that made up a full frame. The second big job was to find and transport

54

to the yard a small forest of well-curved Devon oak logs for the framing.

The shipwrights took each mold to the pile of logs and selected one of about the right shape. A horizontal power-driven saw with a travelling bed was used to cut slabs off the sides of the log while a band saw cut the rough shape of the inside and outside of the piece of frame. An adz was employed to give the proper finished shape.

For the construction of the new *Mayflower* many old shipbuilding skills and tools had to be dusted off. Vessels requiring the sizes of timber used in her had not been built in Brixham for years but there were still old shipwrights who could handle the tools and young shipwrights and apprentices willing and eager to learn. It was not thought necessary, however, to resurrect the ancient art of pit sawing; power saws were employed as noted above. Another concession to modern times was the use of electric drills although hand augers were employed for many of the holes of which there were thousands. I cannot resist the temptation to say that the use of hand augers can be very boring in hard oak.

By Thanksgiving Day 1955 the ship looked something like the backbone of a fish that one might find on a beach. The stem and inner apron had been set up on the forward end of the keel and most of the floor timbers were in place. By the end of the year the first of the frames were erected and the vessel, with her curious bulges, looked much like the skeleton of a whale. At the time of my third trip to Brixham in April 1956 the framing had been completed to the upper deck and the lower deck clamps were in place. On the outside of the hull the lower of the two heavy wales had been fitted and there were eight strakes of oak planking beneath it.

There is much more to shipbuilding than just constructing the hull hence many other items had to be considered and work started on them, too, so that they would be ready to go into the ship at the proper time. Among these items were the masts and yards for which no suitable timber could be found in England. Special Douglas fir logs were obtained and shipped over from British Columbia.

Progress on the hull continued steadily through the summer of 1956 working toward a launching date in September. When thinking of a launching several pictures come to mind – a brilliant day, a pretty lady breaking a ribbon-bedecked bottle on the stem, a slow majestic slide into the water with great waves washing around, and finally, fussy little tugs shepherding the new ship into her outfitting berth. The new *Mayflower*, complete to the lower deck, was launched at

THE MAYFLOWER

8.00am on Saturday, 22 September 1956, during a rousing thunderstorm, one of the worst that South Devon, a region where thunderstorms are rare, had experienced for some time. According to old folklore this meant that the ship would be lucky and I was told later that in some parts of England people had prayed for a thunderstorm that morning.

A public address system installed in the Upham yard for the occasion succumbed early to the storm hence the service of dedication and speeches by those connected closely with the project were lost to all but the few guests around the speakers' platform under the ship's great stem. All, however, joined in the hymns 'O God of Jacob' and 'Abide with Me' which were echoed by the crowds on the quays and house-tops of Brixham across the harbor.

The launching ceremony followed seventeenth-century practice in which the sponsor was a man, in this case one who had done something dramatic for Anglo-American relations, Reis Leming from Yakima in the State of Washington. While serving in the United States Air Force and stationed in England he saved twenty-seven British lives during the serious east coast floods in 1953 for which he was awarded the George Medal by Queen Elizabeth II. The seventeenth-century sponsor did not smash a bottle on the ship's stem but drank a toast to her from a wine-filled standing gilt cup, spilled a little on the deck as he named her, and then heaved the cup into the water. A hardy swimmer usually went in after the cup and sold it back to the master shipwright. For the new *Mayflower* the ceremony was expanded so that Stuart Upham and all the shipwrights who had worked on the ship joined in drinking the toast from a silver goblet after which it was thrown into Brixham harbor. A hardy swimmer, Beric Watson – a future member of the crew – went after the goblet and then, only slightly wetter than most of the guests, presented it to Mary Ann, Reis Leming's charming wife, as a memento of the occasion.

Then came the crucial time. On each side of the ship ten shipwrights with mauls commenced driving in wedges, three to each man, to transfer the ship's weight from the keel blocks to the launching ways, all done in time to a chant sung in the old manner by George Phillips, Foreman Shipwright:

> One blow, two blow, three blow
> Strike her hard, strike her hard
> Inch a blow, up she go
> One blow, two blow, three blow.

THE MAYFLOWER

After a rest the process was repeated until the supporting shores and keel blocks could be knocked out. Iron safety dogs holding the sliding ways to the standing ways were removed and when Stuart Upham counted 'one-two-three', a single spur shore on each side was knocked clear.

With no hesitation the new *Mayflower* slipped down the ways, gave a graceful curtsy as she took to the water and skittered out across the harbor, scattering a fleet of small sightseeing boats and yachts. The band of the Somerset Light Infantry played 'The Battle Hymn of the Republic' while three cheers were called and given with gusto by the crowd. There were few dry eyes among those closely connected with the project as the ship floated gracefully on the calm waters of Brixham harbor.

As the Upham yard did not have a suitable outfitting pier, immediately after launching a small diesel-propelled lighter pushed the ship into the yard's small drydock for completion. By the week before Christmas 1956 the upper deck was finished, the superstructures framed, and the foremast stepped. The upper works were completed and the other masts stepped by the end of February 1957. During the completion of the structure the yard's riggers were hard at work making up the various items so as to be ready when the masts were stepped. All the rope was lightly tarred Italian hemp specially spun by the Gourock Ropeworks Company Ltd, of Port Glasgow, Scotland. There were cable-laid stays, four-stranded shrouds, and tapered tacks in addition to quantities of regular three-stranded rope. The riggers had to worm, parcel, and serve portions of the shrouds and stays, fit leather protection at points of wear, make innumerable eyes and seize in a multitude of blocks and deadeyes.

As soon as each mast was stepped its standing rigging was fitted and set up. Next came the yards with all the necessary running rigging and finally the sails were bent. Flax canvas for these came from the looms of Francis Webster and Sons Ltd, of Arbroath, Scotland; incidentally, a 'webster' was a weaver. The sails were cut and hand-sewn by Harold Bridge in his little shop in Brixham. He used number 4 canvas for the fore- and mainsails and the spritsail and number 6 for the topsails and lateen mizzen.

In the outfitting of the new *Mayflower* the basic concept of an historical exhibit was followed as far as possible but the fact that she was to sail across the Atlantic had to be considered. Modern regulations could not be ignored nor could the modern voyagers be expected to live completely in the seventeenth-century manner. The officials of

the British Ministry of Transport were very cooperative and, realizing that some requirements would destroy or at least seriously affect the character of the ship, considered her in the easiest possible category, that of a yacht. They were interested primarily in the lifesaving, fire-fighting, and navigating equipment but they also looked over all the structural and rigging plans and specifications. Because compliance with the Ministry's requirements and the installation of accommodations for the passage would require on-the-job conferences between the inspectors, the ship's master and others, all this special work became the responsibility of the builders.

For the Atlantic crossing the Ministry of Transport required a steering wheel in the open instead of the whipstaff which had been fitted and tested; the wheel was located over the little hatch in the half-deck just forward of the mizzen mast. By 1959 the wheel had been removed and the whipstaff replaced; it proved an effective means of steering when the ship was sailed in Massachusetts Bay in 1964. Two binnacles were fitted for the passage, a modern one near the wheel and an old-fashioned one, forward of that containing a dry-card compass copied from one believed to have been made a little after the original *Mayflower* sailed. Two other reproductions of early seventeenth-century navigating equipment were carried, a cross-staff, the fore-runner of the modern sextant, and a traverse board. Of course, the captain and mates had their own modern sextants for use during the passage.

Another anachronism and requirement of the Ministry was a radio whose batteries were charged daily by a diesel-driven generator. The same batteries served a simple electric lighting system throughout the ship but because of the limited amount of diesel fuel carried the radio and electric lights were used sparingly on the passage. Copies of old candle lanterns were provided for general illumination while the navigation lights had modern oil-burning lamps. The diesel generator, provided by the Lister firm, provided a bit of amusement for those in the know when the ship was in various ports on each side of the Atlantic. After the ship was afloat it was difficult to convince the average visitor that she was propelled entirely by sail. When the noisy exhaust of the diesel echoed across the harbor there were many wise looks and much nodding of heads – 'See, a motor, I told you so!'

For the Atlantic passage the officers and crew were accommodated

X. Mayflower II *in Brixham harbor, preparing for her voyage to the USA, April 1957.* (Popperfoto)

in small temporary cabins each having one or two metal berths, hanging lockers, and such shelves as could be fitted. The exception to this was Captain Villiers who occupied the small cabin on the halfdeck. Most of the crew were quartered on the lower deck where there were bunks for 23 persons. Two men were berthed in the forecastle which also served as the carpenter's shop, boatswain's storeroom, and lamp room. Cabins under the halfdeck had berths for 7 persons.

Perhaps the most important space in the ship was the galley. For the crossing a modern-type galley with an oil-burning range, a small kerosene stove for emergency use, a sink, and the necessary dressers and racks were arranged on the upper deck forward of the great cabin. The latter served as the officers' mess while the crew's mess was located on the stepped-down section of the lower deck under the tiller. The table in the great cabin was made from my drawing by the boys of the Kitwood Secondary Modern School of Boston, Lincolnshire, England, who did a fine job of constructing and 'ageing' it. The additional patina that it received while serving as a mess table makes it look like a rare antique.

The basic color of the above-water hull, variously described as amber, buff, or pumpkin, was supposed to represent the color of Stockholm tar on oak planking. Stockholm tar is a good preservative but it takes a long time to dry and it was feared that visitors would end up better tarred than the ship; it also picks up dirt and with additional coats and age turns dark brown. The late Captain Sam Svensson, then curator of Sweden's National Maritime Museum in Stockholm, suggested the coating applied, a normal paint based on a 50/50 mixture of raw sienna and raw umber. This unfortunately weathered to a strange pinkish hue and the hull was a dark brown until 1982 when it was painted a lighter color.

For decoration several of the *Mayflower* models, including Dr Anderson's, and paintings of her and other ships of the period have had several bands of triangles of various colors. An early hull model of the new ship had such decoration but the more I thought about and discussed the subject with others the less suitable it seemed for an ordinary merchant ship. A comment by Dr Anderson concerning ships of 1607 noted that, while triangular patterns might be suitable for that date, he had concluded that they were too old-fashioned for 1620.[15] Decoration with plain bands of color and a few fancy moldings has a long tradition at sea and such a scheme was finally selected. The colors used were the simple ones available in the period – yellow ochre, an earth red, green, blue, oyster white, and black – but how closely they matched the old colors is anyone's guess.

The protection of the underwater part of the hull against marine borers, and growths of various types was and still is a grave problem. In the days of the original ship the bottoms of ships were usually coated with a mixture of tallow, white lead, and sulfur; sometimes ground glass was added to the mixture as further discouragement to the worms. Colorwise the net effect was an off-white when the coating was new. At launching time the new ship had modern white anti-fouling paint on her bottom but before she left the dry dock all but a three-foot boot-topping was coated with a grey-green bottom paint which had better anti-fouling qualities than the white.

In research circles the question has been raised from time to time as to whether a ship of the early seventeenth century would have had her name and port of hail carved or painted on her stern. The consensus favors a 'no' answer but examples to the contrary can be found. The first English law requiring the registration of British-built ships was passed in 1696 while the first requiring a permanent name for a vessel and the painting of it on her was not enacted until 1786. Agreeing that the new ship was unlikely to be confused with any other afloat the Ministry of Transport officials waived modern regulations on the subject; the ship is identified, however, by a stylized version of the mayflower of the 1600s, the white hawthorn, on her stern.

The available depth of water over the dry dock sill at high tide limited the amount of work that could be done on the ship while in the dock. Many small items could have been done better with the ship in the dry dock than out in the harbor but the major problem was the installation of ballast. As a 'yacht' the new *Mayflower* could not carry cargo in the normal sense but she was to have a hold full of 'Treasure Chests' containing high quality goods of British manufacture for exhibition in the United States. None of these nor the stores could be loaded until all the ballast was in and secured and this could not be done until the ship was afloat although 68 tons of concrete and old rails had been put in the hold.

On the last favorable tide for a two-week period, predicted for about 7.30pm on the evening of Monday, 1 April 1957, the ship was to be taken from the dry dock. By the predicted time the tide was still about 15in shy of predicted height and the ship was not afloat. Most of the side shores had been removed and the builders faced a serious decision – to reset the shores and wait two weeks or to knock out the remaining shores and try to drag the ship off the keel blocks. They elected the second course and when the shores were removed the ship fell to the starboard side. The same little lighter that had pushed her into the dock finally towed her free and she moved out into the harbor and the night rolling considerably with a definite list to starboard. The British press immediately dubbed her the 'Rock-and-Roll' ship and gave her a 50/50 chance of reaching the United States.

Once secured to a mooring it was apparent that the list was caused by a great pile of spare sails, coils of heavy rope, and other gear in the 'tween deck space that had slid to starboard when the ship fell off the blocks. These were restowed and an additional 15 tons of ballast waiting on the quay was put in the hold. When Tuesday morning dawned the new *Mayflower* was riding steadily in Brixham harbor looking like a toy ship on a painted ocean.

On Thursday an inclining experiment was conducted under the supervision of Ministry of Transport officials to determine the final ballasting. The weight of the 'Treasure Chests' proved less than antici-pated and 50 tons of additional ballast – making the total 133 tons – was required to meet the stability requirements.

For the next week and a half a multitude of small things held up sailing trials and the departure for the United States. Each succeeding day, however saw the ship a little deeper in the water and a sail or two set to check on the rigging and familiarize the crew with the proper operations. Finally, on Tuesday, 16 April, at about four o'clock in the afternoon, the little lighter came alongside and with the ship's crew working on the lower deck and in the hold, a preventer anchor chain was hauled in and stowed. The ship was unshackled from the mooring buoy and towed out into Tor Bay for a trial. She was saluted by horns, bells, and cannon and followed by a flotilla of sightseeing boats, fishing boats, and yachts, most of them filled with photographers. My wife had been on one of these all day and during the two hours of the sea trial she was nearly trampled by thirty of the world's best marine photographers as they rushed from bow to stern to get the best shots of the ship, the first photographs of the new *Mayflower* under full sail.

As the ship passed the end of Brixham's outer breakwater her sails were set one by one – first the courses, after which the towline was cast off, then the topsails, the spritsail, and finally the lateen mizzen – and she proceeded to confound the critics. She made about 4½kts in a 10kt breeze, sailed close-hauled about 6 points off the wind, and tacked in about 3 minutes without losing way. These things I know, for I was on board and at the wheel for nearly an hour. Among the crew that

XI. *Stern view in Brixham harbor during the fitting out period, April 1957.* (Author)

day was Britain's most 'extraordinary ordinary' seaman, the late Sir Alan Moore, Bart., who, at the end of the trial, was found on the fore yard helping furl the sail in company with the 16-year-old cabin boy, Graham Nunn, 60 years his junior.

That, sketchily, is the story of the designing and building of the new *Mayflower* that is now on exhibition at Plymouth, Massachusetts; the story of the trans-Atlantic passage properly belongs to those who made it. When Warwick Charlton, founder of the British group that sponsored the building of the ship, started his project there were those who said that plans could not be obtained, but they were. Then came statements that the ship could not be built, but she was. Lastly, the critics said that she would not sail, but she did and crossed the Atlantic, weathering a 50kt gale with ease. The new *Mayflower* proved that early seventeenth-century shipbuilders and seamen were competent, but she has also shown why there have been improvements in the design, construction, and rigging of sailing ships.

XII. *A rigging detail of* Mayflower II. (Author)

CHAPTER 3

Small Craft –
The Pilgrims' Shallop

Let us assume that we are sailing from England to the New World of New England at the beginning of the fourth decade of the seventeenth century. What types of vessels can we expect to find there? The ships will be mainly of English build although a few have been constructed in the colonies; in 1641 a 300-ton ship will be launched at Gloucester on Cape Ann. The smaller vessels and boats will be of types familiar at home but not in the great variety to be found in the ports of a long established economy. As gleaned from many sources we can expect to see shallops, pinnaces, and barks in profusion; a fair number of catches (or ketches), many small boats and lighters, and an occasional galliot, hoy, and Dutch sloop.

Arriving off the New England coast, say near Cape Ann, early one morning in the summer of 1641 we see a number of small fishing boats, some under sail and some at anchor with their masts down. These are shallops which leads to the question – 'sloep' in Dutch, 'slup' in Swedish, 'chaloupe' in French, and 'shallop' in English but just what was it? As with many things marine these terms were applied somewhat loosely at any given time.

From many accounts we know that the shallop, along with the pinnace, was a type of boat employed extensively by the early explorers and colonists of the New World. Not only were shallops used by the explorers of whom we have record but the fact that a few were greeted by natives in shallops, in one case under sail, points to more early activity along the New England coast than generally assumed. The craft in native hands were usually Basque or Biscay shallops, the best whaleboats of their day.

The shallops of the explorers and early colonists usually were carried on the larger vessels in some sort of prefabricated or cut-down form – *chaloupe-en-fagot* as the French put it – ready to be put together at their destination. Captain John Smith recorded the arrival of the London Company colonists off Cape Henry at the entrance to Chesapeake Bay in 1607 and continued '. . . so next day we began to build our shallop, which had been shipped in portions, easy to be fitted together'.[1] Referring to the shallop brought over in the *Mayflower* in 1620 Mourt's *Relation* noted:[2]

> Monday, 13 November, we unshipped our shallop and drew her on land to mend and repair her, having been forced to cut her down in bestowing her betwixt the decks, and she was much opened with the people lying in her, which kept us long there, for it was sixteen or seventeen days before the carpenter had finished her.

It is worth noting that while the carpenter was thus busy some of the colonists were employed in cutting timber for another shallop.

John Brereton, who was on Bartholomew Gosnold's expedition to New England in 1602, left a confusing reference to a shallop '. . . we hoisted out the one half of our shallop, and Captain Bartholomew Gosnold, myself and three others, went ashore . . . so returning towards evening to our shallop (for by that time the other part was brought ashore and set together. . .)'. There is no definite information as to how these halves of a shallop were constructed or of the method of joining the two into a complete boat.[3]

The obvious place to look for a definition or description of a shallop would be an old marine dictionary. Turning to the earliest English one, Sir Henry Mainwaring's *The Seaman's Dictionary* of about 1620, we find that 'shallop' is not listed but under 'boat' is the following:

> The boat belonging to a ship is either called the ship's boat or the long boat. . . Other small boats which they carry for lightness to hoist in and out quickly, are called skiffs or shallops, according to form. . . A ship's boat is the very model of a ship and is built with parts in all things answerable to those which a ship requires, both for sailing and bearing a sail. . .

This is not very helpful, for under 'skiff' Mainwaring simply refers back to 'boat' but we can note that *form* had something to do with defining a shallop. In January 1627 the English ship *Prince Royal* had 'one shallop for ye harbour' that was 27ft long, 6ft 9in wide, and 2ft 4in deep.

Randle Cotgrave's *A Dictionarie of the French and English Tongues* published in London in 1611 defines *chaloupe* as a shallop or small boat and an *esquif* as a skiff or little boat. For later French definitions we can look at the *Dictionaire du Gentilhomme* by le Sieur Guillet, published in The Hague in 1686, and Aubin's *Dictionaire de*

THE PILGRIMS' SHALLOP

Marine, a French work with Dutch equivalents published in Amsterdam in 1702, which have essentially the same definitions. The following is from Guillet:

> Chaloupe est un petit bâtiment propre a des traversées & destiné au service & à la communication des grands vaisseaux. Canot est un esquif ou petit Batteau pour le service d'un grand Bâtiment. Esquif est un petit batteau pour le service d'un Navire.

From this we can see that the 'chaloupe' was the largest of the three types of small craft described, was capable of making coastwise passages, and in general performed the duties of what today might be called a tender. A rough size definition might be that it was an open boat just a bit too big to be carried conveniently on all but the largest ships. It was perhaps the equivalent of Mainwaring's long boat while the 'canot' was the same as his shallop.

About the earliest printed plans of shallops were published along with several descriptions in Nicolaes Witsen's great work on shipbuilding in 1671, *Aeloude en Hedendaegsche Scheeps-Bouw en Bestier.* In the absence of copyright laws in those days there was much plagiarism and the material was copied widely. Aubin did not include the plans in his *Dictionaire* but translated into French the descriptions of two 'sloops' or shallops. The first was a double-ender 32ft long with a beam of 8ft 9in while the second was a transom-sterned craft having a length of 42ft 4in and a breadth of 9ft. The former was fitted with one mast and leeboards while the latter had two masts with square sails but there was no mention of leeboards.

Other descriptions and dimensions might be cited but there is little to be gained by just piling up details hence we will turn to a few users' reports. Captain John Smith mentioned many expeditions for exploration and trade in the shallop carried to Virginia by the Jamestown colonists but left no clues as to its size or construction. His map of Chesapeake Bay showed a single-masted double-ended craft, presumably this shallop, in one of the upper reaches of the bay.

Concerning the shallop brought over in the *Mayflower* there are two sources of information, Mourt's *Relation* from which a passage has already been quoted and Governor Bradford's journal *Of Plimoth Plantation* (actually two versions by the same writer). To compare with the passage from the *Relation*, Bradford mentioned that the shallop was stowed in quarters in the ship and was 'much bruised and shattered in the ship with foul weather'. When eighteen of the *Mayflower*'s company finally set out in the repaired shallop to explore the shores of

THE PILGRIMS' SHALLOP

Cape Cod looking for a suitable location for settling Mourt stated '. . . [we] got up our sails'. Later, when the craft was caught in a storm off the Gurnet, the Headland at the end of the long sand spit that encloses Duxbury Bay, he noted 'we split our mast in three pieces'. Referring to the same situation Bradford wrote in his journal 'they bore what sail they could to get in' and 'But herewith they broke their mast in three pieces & their sail fell overboard in a very grown sea'.

Notes concerning other shallops were collected from colonial records and published by John Robinson and George Francis Dow in *The Sailing Ships of New England, 1607–1907* and by Professor E P Morris in *The Fore-and-Aft Rig in America.* On the arrival of Governor Winthrop's ships off Cape Ann, Massachusetts, in 1630 he noted a meeting with a fishing shallop and the next day he received a visitor from a shallop bound for Pemaquid. A great shallop was wrecked on Cape Ann in 1635, a 10-ton shallop capsized in Boston harbor in 1640, and fishing shallops from the Boston region ran into difficulties when returning from Monhegan island in 1648. In court records for 1675 there is a valuation of a shallop having masts, yards, fore- and mainsails, and rigging that was large enough to have its own boat. The settlement at Strawberry Bank (now Portsmouth, New Hampshire) had six great shallops, five fishing boats with sails, anchors, and cables, and thirteen skiffs in 1631.[4]

As might be expected the notes refer more to the rig and handling of shallops than to form and construction. Professor Morris interpreted the problem as follows:

> Postponing for a moment the question of rig, the other characteristics harmonize easily; the shallop, having come over as a ship's boat, had become a type, an open craft, probably square sterned, of a size between the small rowboat and the decked vessel. The hesitation of Bradford between 'boat' and 'shallop' shows that size was an element in the meaning, and the use of the terms 'great shallop', 'double shallop', or craft as large as a pinnace shows that the typical form also was necessary.

Concerning rig, Professor Morris noted, in addition to the *Mayflower* items given above, the following that seems to indicate a single mast:

> . . . one of the three 'ancient and skillful seamen' whose shallop was capsized 'had the sheet in his hand and let fly'; 'hoisted part of their sail'; 'to hand the sail. . .'

XIII. Mayflower II *carrying out sailing trials, 16 April 1957.* (Plimoth Plantation, Inc)

THE MAYFLOWER

After which he added:

> But the passage from the *New Haven Colonial Records*, 'to have cast her by flatting her foresayle', is conclusive proof that the shallop sometimes had two masts. . .

There are a number of definite references to two masts in shallop descriptions of the latter part of the seventeenth century.

In spite of such researches into colonial records by many historians and naval architects we do not have a clear picture of an early colonial shallop; it is, in fact, almost easier to say what a shallop was not. Lengthening and decking over could convert a shallop to a pinnace but this is part of another story. By the middle of the seventeenth century the typical shallops were open double-ended boats propelled by oars and sails. The colonial shallop's descendants in comparatively recent times were such well known New England craft as the Hampton boat, the Crotch Island pinky, the No man's Land boat, and the Block Island boat.[5]

Since March 1957 another shallop has been sailing in waters near the Gurnet, thus far without her mast splitting in three pieces and her sails falling over the side. Her lines are shown in Figs 10 and 11 while Fig 12 is a sketch of her under sail.

The first step in preparing plans for this craft was, of course, to survey the available pictorial and written material on shallops. The results of this survey are summarized above. The bulk of the material available to me indicated the craft shown in the plans and sketch – a heavily constructed double-ended open boat having one mast with a sprit mainsail and what we usually call a jib.

Double-ended hulls of the type shown can be found in old drawings, engravings, and paintings at least as far back as the reign of Henry VIII of England. Plans of similar hulls of the first half of the seventeenth century can be found in European libraries and museums. Small craft of essentially the same form and construction can be found in European waters today. Construction details, therefore, offered no great problem.

The form of the hull was more of a problem. No complete lines plan for a small boat of the early seventeenth century has been found to date but some existing plans show three sections from which reasonable approximations can be developed. As stated above there are present day small craft closely resembling those of the seventeenth century hence the use of lines based on them is reasonable.

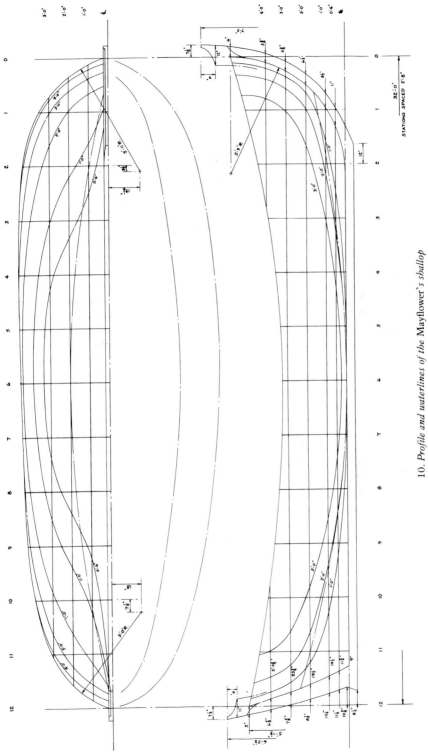

10. *Profile and waterlines of the Mayflower's shallop*

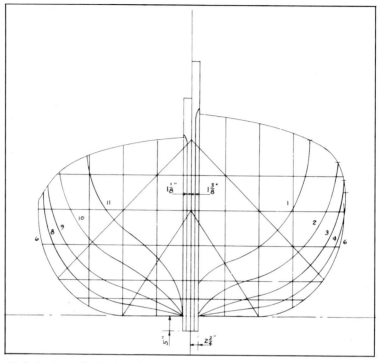

11. *Body plan of the* Mayflower's *shallop*

The rig of one mast with sprit mainsail and jib was chosen as it is the only rig consistently shown in old drawings, engravings, and paintings from several countries over a span of at least two hundred years. As the *Mayflower*'s shallop hoisted 'sails' on one mast two sails were required and there are only scattered examples of a square sail with a jib or two square sails on one mast. If, as Professor Morris argued, the presence of a 'foresayle' can be taken as conclusive proof of a two-masted rig it is equally conclusive proof of a rig with but one mast. The sail that today we call the jib in our standard 'jib-and-mainsail' sloop rig was originally, and still is to the English, the foresail. The sprit mainsail has a practical quality in that its area may be cut roughly in half simply by dropping the sprit and securing the peak to the tack of the sail. This procedure leaves a snug triangular sail and the use of a sail in such a condition may explain the phrase mentioned earlier: 'hoisted part of their sail'.

Perhaps the most difficult problem was the size of the new shallop. Eighteen men, food and water, arms, and presumably some blankets comprised the load of the *Mayflower*'s shallop for the exploration trip along the shores of Cape Cod. According to one interpretation of a passage in Mourt's *Relation* about thirty-two persons were in the shallop on an earlier occasion at which time there must have been sufficient room to handle the sails and oars. The dimensions as finally worked out are length overall 33ft 3in, breadth 9ft 2in, and depth amidships 3ft 3in.

One might argue from the material cited that leeboards were exclusively a Dutch feature. If so, who can deny the possibility that the Pilgrims purchased a Dutch 'sloep'? On the other hand, several English port views, including Visscher's of London mentioned in the first chapter, definitely show small single-masted craft fitted with leeboards.

The new shallop was constructed by the Plymouth Marine Railways Inc of Plymouth, Massachusetts. Her keel was laid with proper ceremonies on 19 January 1957 and her launching on 16 March also took place during a rainstorm. She was christened *Pilgrim Shallop II* by Mrs Foster Furcolo, wife of the then Governor of the Commonwealth of Massachusetts. Once afloat the shallop was rowed around the harbor by Harvard University's varsity crew who found her somewhat heavier than their usual eight-oared shell.

12. *The* Mayflower's *shallop under sail*

73

THE MAYFLOWER

The *Pilgrim Shallop II* was under sail for the first time, although with temporary rigging, on Sunday 17 March, when several hundred visitors to Plymouth were taken out in small groups for trips around the harbor. On 13 June 1957, the new shallop, under the command of George S Davis of Plymouth and with a crew of Pilgrim descendants, served to bring Captain Alan Villiers and his crew ashore from the *Mayflower II* at the end of their 54-day passage from Plymouth, England.

At the beginning of August 1958 the shallop and a crew of modern Pilgrims under the command of Edward Rowe Snow, the historian from Marshfield, Massachusetts, re-enacted portions of two of the early trips of the original shallop. Following a tow that resembled a 'Nantucket sleigh-ride' from Plymouth to Provincetown at the tip of Cape Cod, the shallop sailed south along the shore to Wellfleet where the first night was spent. On the second day she made a passage across Massachusetts Bay to Clark's Island in Duxbury Bay where the Pilgrims had held their first religious service. In the afternoon of the same day she sailed up to Scituate harbor for the second night. The *Pilgrim Shallop II* proceeded to Quincy on Sunday 3 August, where she was a featured exhibit in the marine parade that opened the 1958 Quincy Bay Race Week. This portion of the trip re-traced one of the early expeditions of Captain Miles Standish to Squantum, now the northern part of Quincy. Since then the shallop has been employed at various times in other re-enactments; she is normally moored alongside the *Mayflower II.*

The new shallop with her unfamiliar looking rig and leeboards amuses many modern yachtsmen until they attempt to sail by her. On a reach in a 10kt to 12kt breeze she has been timed between buoys at 5kts although she has but 350 sq ft of working canvas, and no light sails. In heavier winds she has reached 8kts on occasion. When sailing to windward there is little if any difference between her pointing ability and that of many modern craft that have sailed along with her from time to time.

If the *Pilgrim Shallop II* is not a near sister of the one brought over on the *Mayflower* in 1620 there were many similar craft afloat in the early seventeenth century and she would have been no stranger to seafaring people. Sailing in by the Gurnet and beating into Plymouth harbor against the summer south-westerly, is it mere fancy that senses on the helm the hand of Thomas English, master of the *Mayflower*'s shallop?

CHAPTER 4

On Pinnaces

And finding they rane a great hazard to goe so long viages in a smale open boat, espetially ye winter season, they begane to thinke how they might get a small pinass . . . tooke one of ye bigest of ther shalops and sawed her in ye midle, and so lenthened her some 5 or 6 foote, and strengthened her with timbers, and so builte her up, and laid a deck on her; and so made her a conveniente, and wholesome vessell, very fitt & comfortable for their use, which did them servise 7 years after . . .

With these words Governor William Bradford described the maritime plight of the Plymouth colonists in 1626 and what was done to remedy it.[1] Here we have an open *boat*, a shallop that had definite form characteristics, converted by lengthening, deepening, and the fitting of a deck into a pinnace, a *vessel* more suitable for extended operations.

The pinnace category is perhaps the most confusing of all the early seventeenth-century vessel types. Pinnaces ranged from small open pulling boats, some of which were transported in knocked-down form in the same manner as shallops, to relatively large seagoing vessels that carried the normal ship rig of the period. The type name is derived through the French *pinasse* from the Latin *pinus*, meaning a pine tree or something constructed of pine, thus suggesting a lightly-built vessel in contrast to the more or less standard heavy oak construction of the large merchant and war ships. In England and the northern part of France it also points to a craft derived from Scandinavia where pine trees were abundant. Such a craft would have had lapped strakes of planking and is variously known as clench-, clincher-, or clinker-built, the latter being the usual choice today. At least two sources corroborate this theory. In Hakluyt's account of John Davis's third voyage in search of the Northwest passage in 1587, the 'clincher' *Helene* of London is referred to several times as a 'pinnesse'.[2] Oppenheim noted that two pinnaces of Charles I, the *Henrietta* and *Maria* of

1626, were specifically ordered to be built with carvel (smooth) planking.[3] This indicates that clinker planking was then common on small vessels but it is unreasonable to conclude that all pinnaces were clinker-built.

Mainwaring's *The Seaman's Dictionary* has nothing on pinnaces but Boteler noted that there was 'no difference between a ship and a pinnace but in bulk and burthen'. Dutch drawings of the mid-1600s show that a 'pinnasschip' had but one deck with the normal forecastle, and after superstructure of the larger ships. In his *Dictionaire du Gentilhomme* of 1686 le Sieur Guillet stated, as translated into reasonable English, that a pinnace was:

> . . . a small vessel with a square stern which is propelled by sails and oars and which has three masts. It is suitable for exploring and for landing troops.

Aubin's *Dictionaire de Marine*, 1702, had two definitions of *pinasse* which, again in reasonable English, are:

> . . . is a vessel built with a square stern which originated in the North, and which is used extensively in Holland. It is believed that it is called 'Pinus', pine, because the first pinnaces were built of pine. . . . it is a small Biscayan vessel that has a square stern. It is long, narrow, and light, which makes it suitable for privateering, exploring, and for landing people on a coast. It has three masts and is propelled by sails and oars.

Over a hundred years earlier Mathew Baker wrote in his notebook that a chart giving the breadths of a vessel at several points, including the transom, could be used for a pinnace as well as a ship thus corroborating the square stern. Recorded dimensions of English vessels show that the typical pinnaces were narrower for their lengths than other types of vessels.

It is obvious that a light vessel fitted with oars as well as sails – at least enough oar-power to move around a harbor and in calms but not for steady propulsion in galley fashion – would be useful as a tender to a large ship in addition to the activities mentioned above. We have noted that a 'chaloupe' was a type of tender and suitable for short voyages. But even small pinnaces, other than the open pulling boats, were enough larger to be capable of making ocean voyages of considerable duration. Accounts of sixteenth- and seventeenth-century voyages are full of references to ships and their accompanying pinnaces which in some cases were quite large.

It is apparent that a small vessel, intended to sail in company with a larger ship, must have had a form and rig that enabled it, under normal conditions, to keep up with the ship. Not all pinnaces were capable of this and often they were towed. Leaving until later the question of rig the form requirement indicates a narrower beam in relation to length and a finer shape; enough material on large pinnaces is available to prove these two points.

As a general observation we might say that almost any vessel could have been designated as the pinnace to accompany a larger one. In other words, while 'pinnace' started as a name derived from constructional features, it came in many cases to indicate a use or service. The situation is confused, however, by the fact that pinnaces often voyaged alone.

The Plymouth colonists had some rather unfortunate experiences with pinnaces which are mentioned about fourteen times in Governor Bradford's journal. The first noted – but not by name – was the *Speedwell* which was purchased in Holland and, after carrying settlers to the New World, was expected to serve the colonists for fishing and trading ventures. There is no need here to go into the frustrations caused by her leaks and the final decision of the colonists to leave her in England.

In the summer of 1623 a new pinnace of about 44 tons arrived at the Plymouth colony. Called the *Little James* she had been built for the company of merchant adventurers backing the colonists and was intended to handle the duties for which the *Speedwell* had been destined. It is obvious that but a few of her coastwise activities were recorded – then as now it was the catastrophes that made the news. In 1623, on her return from a trip around Cape Cod to trade with the Narragansett Indians, she was nearly cast away on the flats off Brown's Island at the entrance to Plymouth harbor when her anchors dragged. Her mainmast was cut away and the reduced windage enabled her anchors to catch and hold. At considerable time and expense the mast was replaced and the pinnace re-rigged by the next year.

In 1624, the *Little James* was sent to the eastward, the coast of Maine, to fish. While anchored in a harbor near Damariscove she was hit by another storm which 'drive her againste great roks, which beat such a hole in her bulke, as a horse and carte might have gone in, and after drive her into deep water wher she lay sunke'. The pinnace eventually was raised and repaired but the cost caused the colony's officials to consider her too expensive and she was sent back to England.

For the second time the plantation was deprived of a small vessel for fishing and trading and was forced to rely on its open shallops. Some

XIV. Mayflower II *under full sail in calm weather, October 1964.* (Author)

sort of a decked vessel was needed and the colonists resorted to the procedure described at the beginning of this chapter. In 1627 a small pinnace was built at the head of Buzzards Bay for use in connection with the trading post at Aptucxet; a re-creation of this establishment now stands near the south bank of the Cape Cod canal.

References to pinnaces in the *History of New England* by Governor John Winthrop of the Massachusetts Bay Colony are concerned mainly with trading voyages, wrecks, and the activities of the French on the coast of Maine where they attacked the small fishing settlements and trading posts. There are references to 'open' pinnaces, to 'small' pinnaces ranging from 10 to 30 tons in size, and to a 50-tonner, the largest mentioned.

Winthrop noted a variety of trading voyages but these probably were only a small part of the total activity; each may have been the first of its type. In 1631 an 18-ton pinnace arrived at Salem, Massachusetts, from Virginia loaded with corn and tobacco. The *Dove*, the 50-tonner mentioned above, came from Maryland in 1634 with corn to exchange for fish and other commodities. Heifers and goats from Virginia formed a pinnace's cargo in 1636 while in 1642 two pinnaces arrived at Boston from Maryland to buy mares and sheep. In August 1643 a Boston pinnace loaded coal on John's River in what is now Canada's Province of New Brunswick.

The references in Winthrop's *History* to 'open' pinnaces are confusing as the definitions given earlier require a deck. A survey of small craft made in 1627 indicates that a pulling pinnace was about the same size as the 'shallop for ye harbour' mentioned in the previous chapter, the pinnace being one foot longer, three inches wider, and four inches deeper. Considering that the definitions of pinnaces emphasize the square stern, we can assume that this was the difference between the shallop and the small open pinnace – the former was a double-ender while the latter had a transom stern. In view of this the result of the shallop conversion described in the first paragraph would not have been a true pinnace but, all things considered, there was no other convenient category.

Turning now to the question of rig, we have noted that almost any vessel might have been chosen as the 'pinnace' for a larger one hence there must have been pinnaces with a variety of rigs. The conditions of service probably influenced the choice of rig, that selected for coastwise work differing from that for a deep-sea voyage. Portraits of vessels with contemporary designations as pinnaces are few but sufficient to substantiate these statements.

THE MAYFLOWER

In Chapter 3 we considered a shallop with one mast that carried a sprit mainsail and a jib or staysail. Lengthening such a shallop the five or six feet described by Governor Bradford would not have been sufficient reason to change the rig especially considering the economic condition of the Plymouth colony at the time. Researchers generally agree that there is at least one portrait of a pinnace so rigged.

In 1607 the Plymouth Company, which with the London (or Virginia) Company had received a royal charter in 1606, sent out on expedition under the command of George Popham that established a short lived colony at the mouth of the Sagadahoc (Kennebec) River on the coast of Maine. Among the colonists was a shipwright, one Digby of London, and 'he and the carpenters framed a pretty Pynnace of about thirty tons, which they called the Virginia. . .' in the words of William Strachey, the Virginia Company's first secretary, from his *History of Travell into Virginia Britania*. A map of Popham's colony labelled 'St Georges Fort', found in the Spanish Archives in the late 1800s, clearly showed a small but substantial square-sterned vessel rigged with one mast carrying a sprit mainsail and a staysail; a scale on the map establishes her overall length at about 50ft. Fig 13 is a redrawing of this sketch.

13. *Vessel at St Georges fort, Sagadahoc, 1607*

ON PINNACES

While there is nothing on the map to identify this vessel as the *Virginia*, the other vessels known to have been at Sagadahoc were larger. The fore-and-aft rig shown would have been handy in poking into the multitude of rivers, bays, and coves along the coast of the present State of Maine and for occasional voyages to the Jamestown colony in Virginia. Coastwise passages from Maine to Virginia are practically always long beats against the prevailing south-west wind for which a square-rig is ill suited. When the Popham colony was abandoned in 1608 the *Virginia* carried some of the colonists back to England; she returned to the New World in 1609, one of a fleet of nine vessels that carried more than 600 Jamestown-bound colonists.

A modern re-creation of the *Virginia* in miniature, commissioned by the Bath Iron Works Corporation, is now on exhibition in the Bath (Maine) Marine Museum. From preliminary sketches of her lines and rig that I drew, Carl M Langbehn of Bath developed the detail plans and built an excellent model to the scale of ½in = 1ft. The basic dimensions of this *Virginia* are: Keel length 38ft 6in, breadth 13ft, and depth 6ft. The overall length worked out to 51ft 6in. For her simple rig the staysail measured 250 sq ft and the sprit main 880 sq ft, giving a total sail area of 1130 sq ft.

In Chapter 3 we argued that certain passages in colonial records proved that shallops carried a single-masted fore-and-aft rig but there is no question that there were also shallops rigged with one or two masts carrying square sails only. The Biscay shallop normally carried a two-masted square rig that became popular for fishing boats and small coasters throughout northern Europe. The Dutch in particular made great use of it, the various types of 'pinks' widely employed by the fishermen who worked off the North Sea beaches being well known examples.

The Biscay shallop's rig was unusual in that the mainmast, stepped practically amidships, carried a large square sail while the foremast, stepped in the very eyes of the boat, had a small square sail that was roughly one quarter of the main in area. Both sails were relatively deep and narrow. Because of its location the small foresail was not usually set when the shallop was beating to windward unless the shallop had a bowsprit to which bowlines could be led or a portable spar to support the leech of the sail as shown in Fig 16. On other points of sailing both sails were employed. Fig 14 shows a small Dutch 'pink' working to windward under her mainsail. While there is evidence that the area of the mainsail could be reduced in heavy weather, by removing a bonnet in early versions and later by tying in a reef, in a severe storm

XV. *Model of* Pilgrim Shallop II, *by M M Gidley.* (Author)

ON PINNACES

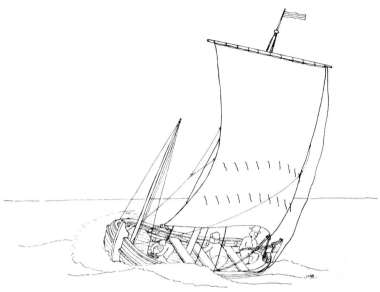

14. *Dutch 'pink' – after van de Velde*

the mainmast could be unstepped and replaced by the foremast and its small sail. Through many ramifications this basic rig developed on one hand into the many variations of the lug rig that were so prominent along the British and French coasts and, on the other, to the full-rigged brig.

Portrayals of early seagoing two-masted square-riggers are rare but three are shown in Lucas Janszoon Waghenaer's *Spieghel der Zee-vaerdt* of 1584, a series of charts of the coasts of northern Europe. Their rigs appear to be developments of that of the Biscay shallop. One has the round or 'pink' stern of the period and both her masts can carry topsails. As shown in Fig 15 she is carrying fore and main courses and the main topsail; the absence of the fore topsail yard indicates the possibility that the topsails were set flying from the deck. The other two vessels seem to have square sterns and their rigs maintain the basic proportions of the Biscay shallop rig in that there is no provision for a fore topsail.

The smallest of the three vessels in the 1607 Jamestown fleet was the 20-ton pinnace *Discovery*. A painting by Griffith Baily Coale, now in the Capitol of Virginia in Richmond, depicting the arrival of the fleet off Jamestown on 13 May 1607 shows her as a square-sterned two-masted square-rigger without topsails. The sailing reproduction

15. *Two-masted square-rigged vessel, 1584 – after Waghenaer*

built for the 1957 Jamestown Festival was based on this painting.[4]

The buss, of which many are shown in Waghenaer's work, was widely employed in the early seventeenth-century fishing industry, particularly for herring. The hull form of the buss – bluff bow, full quarters, narrow poop, and practically no overhangs – changed but little from the sixteenth to the nineteenth century. Her normal rig consisted of three pole masts carrying deep narrow square sails with perhaps a small topsail on the main only; there was no bowsprit. A typical buss under full sail is shown in Fig 16. While lying to her drifting nets, the fore- and mainmasts of a buss were lowered and she rode with her small square mizzen set.

ON PINNACES

16. *Typical herring buss*

Sometime during the development of large two-masters the construction and rigging of the foremast was changed to that of the contemporary ship. The fore course was wide and shallow compared with that of the Biscay shallop or buss and the topsail was of substantial size. The mainmast, often a single pole, retained the deep narrow buss-type mainsail. With a few other sails, as shown in Fig 17, such a rig was carried in the late seventeenth century by vessels called brigantines; earlier they might have been known as pinnaces.

The portrait of another two-masted pinnace exists as a ceiling decoration in Hook House which is located in the Parish of Senley, Chalk Hundred, adjacent to Wardour Castle in Wiltshire, England. In 1628, Anne Arundell, daughter of Sir Thomas Arundell, Baron of Wardour, married Cecil Calvert who later became the second Lord Baltimore. Hook Farm was her marriage portion and while living there the couple planned the colonization of Maryland. During repairs in the early 1950s to 'Lady Anne's Sitting Room', a false ceiling was removed revealing a beautifully modeled plaster ceiling commemorating the passage of the ship *Ark* and the pinnace *Dove* to Maryland with colonists in 1633. This ceiling is not dated but the initials 'AA' and 'CC' in one of the panels would indicate that it was executed before Anne's death thus placing it between 1633 and 1649 and probably before 1643 when Cromwell's men besieged the castle.

Portraits of the *Ark* and the *Dove* are repeated diagonally in the centers of the corner panels of the ceiling; Figs 18 and 19 are outline

THE MAYFLOWER

17. *Brigantine, late seventeenth century*

drawings of these plaster relief portraits. Concerning them M V Brewington wrote:

> The discovery of the four reliefs representing the *Ark* and the *Dove* is an event of very considerable importance to maritime historians and archaeologists. First of all, these are the *only known contemporary representations* of any of the many vessels which brought the original settlers to the British North American colonies. . . Of the *Ark* as depicted on the ceiling little needs to be said. She evidently was a typical ship-rigged vessel of her period, perhaps with a somewhat larger quantity of carved decorations than usual. . . More important is the representation of the *Dove*. While the type of vessel known as a pinnace played an important part in the explorations and the settling of the Atlantic Coast, exactly what the seagoing pinnace (as opposed to those used on the coast or in protected waters) may have been, has never been established definitely. An engraving a half-century before the *Dove* shows one rigged as a three-masted ship, but the pinnaces used by Claiborne and sundry others coasting or within the [Chesapeake] Bay we know were small craft, one-masted, fore-and-aft rigged. Other pinnaces were nothing more than row boats, perhaps with an auxiliary sailing rig. Since the *Dove* is clearly depicted as a two-masted, square-rigged craft, one concludes that the pinnace was rigged according to size as the builder chose, and the name belonged to the hull rather than the rig. . .

After the two-masters in the *Spieghel der Zeevaerdt* we are hardly prepared for this *Dove*. She has a substantial superstructure aft, which

18. *Ship* Ark, *1633*

19. *Pinnace* Dove, *1633*

would be expected, but she also has a prominent forecastle. Each of her masts carries what may be interpreted as a single square sail and she has a bowsprit. Her forward mast has crosstrees or a top but nothing is shown on the other. The artist may have been trying to show something like the brigantine mentioned a few paragraphs earlier.

Let us leave the *Dove* for a moment, return to the lengthened Pilgrim shallop and the *Virginia* of Sagadahoc, and take another look at Waghenaer. In converting a shallop to a pinnace and retaining the single-masted fore-and-aft rig there is a strong possibility that the resulting vessel might be under-canvassed and the rig no longer in balance with the hull. By way of correction it would be simple to add a small lateen mizzen and a bowsprit with a square sail under it; the same steps could be taken when rigging a new vessel. Regardless of how such a rig developed, it and many variations are shown on Baltic and North Sea charts in the *Spieghel der Zeevaerdt* as well as in many port scenes of the early seventeenth century.

20. *Normal bojort – after Waghenaer*

21. *'Square' bojort – after Waghenaer*

In northern European waters vessels having this two-masted rig, with perhaps a square topsail added, carried a name something like the Dutch 'boyer'; the spelling naturally varied from country to country. It was 'bojort' in Sweden where there were regular 'bojorts' and 'square bojorts' on which the sprit mainsail was replaced by a deep narrow square sail which was more suitable for deep-sea voyages. An ordinary 'bojort' is shown in Fig 20 and a 'square bojort' in Fig 21. Zettersen, a Swedish writer, noted in 1896 that there was considerable variation in type names and that a given vessel might have been referred to indiscriminately by several names. Among examples cited, a 'bojort' was referred to as a 'pinnace'.

I see a strong possibility that the artist who molded Lady Anne's ceiling was trying to portray the *Dove* as a 'square bojort' or whatever the English may have called it. From details of the *Ark* it is obvious that the artist was not familiar with ships in general. The second mast on the *Dove* is obviously the smaller and a lateen sail with a bonnet had a definite rectangular shape that such an artist might easily exaggerate into something approximating a square sail.

The largest type of pinnace carried the normal three-masted ship rig of the period; examples of this type can be found over a range of at least 128 years. In 1546 one Anthony Anthony portrayed the fleet of King Henry VIII of England dividing it into four basic types – ships, galleases, pinnaces, and row-barges. One vessel did not qualify for any of these categories, the *Galley Subtylle*, a true Mediterranean-type galley launched in 1545. While some of the vessels seem a little improbable to our eyes, there are enough differences between them to indicate that Anthony tried to portray each unit of the fleet.

One of the ten pinnaces in the fleet was the 80-ton *Roe* built in 1545. Her hull has little sheer and there are no apparent superstructures forward or aft; below her gunports a row of oarports extends nearly her full length. Only her mainmast has a topsail.

Our next example of a ship-rigged pinnace is found about forty years later, the *Black Pynnes*, which carried the body of Sir Philip Sidney from Holland to England in 1586, shown in Fig 22. Many of her features are hidden by the waist cloths and boarding nettings but it is apparent that she has a short forecastle and poop. Marine paintings for the next half century, primarily of fleet actions, show many small vessels of the same type.

The Jamestown-bound nine-vessel fleet of 1609 mentioned earlier was scattered by a storm and its damaged 'Admirall' (flagship), the *Sea Venture* which carried Sir Thomas Gates who had been appointed governor of the colony of Virginia, was deliberately grounded on Bermuda. The ship's company – about 150 men, women, and children – were landed safely by her boats and quantities of supplies and equipment were recovered. When a decked-over longboat, sent to seek aid in Virginia, failed to return and no aid came, the shipwrecked colonists constructed two small vessels. Both were usually called pinnaces although occasionally the larger was called a ship and the smaller a bark.

Unlike the majority of vessels of the period constructed in established shipyards, the dimensions of these two built in adversity were recorded.[6] Concerning the larger William Strachey wrote:

Shee was fortie foot by the Keele, and nineteene foot broad at the Beame, sixe foote floore, her Rake forward was fourteene foot, her Rake aft from the top of her Post (which was twelve foot long) was three foot, shee was eight foot deepe under her Beame, betweene her Deckes she was foure feet

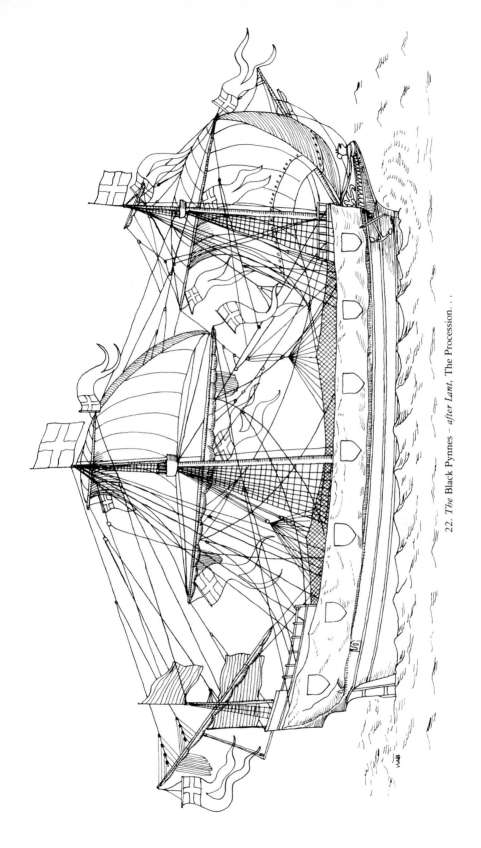

22. *The* Black Pynnes – *after Lant*, The Procession. . .

XVI. *The* Deliverance, *St Georges, Bermuda.* (Author)

and an halfe, with a rising of halfe a foot more under her fore Castle, of purpose to scoure the Decke with small shot, if at any time wee should be borded by the Enemie. Shee had a fall of eighteene inches aft, to make her sterage and her great Cabbin the more large: her sterage was five foot long, and sixe foote high, with a close Gallerie right aft, with a window on each side, and two right aft. . . When shee began to swimme (upon her launching) our Governour called her The Deliverance, and shee might be some eighty tunnes of burthen.

As for the smaller pinnace '. . . shee was by the Keele nine and twentie foot: at the Beame fifteene foot and an halfe: at the Loofe fourteene, at the Transam nine, and she was eight foote deepe, and drew sixe foote water, and hee called her the Patience'.

A dry-land re-creation of the *Deliverance*, sponsored by the Bermuda Junior Service League and built under the supervision of the late Captain Ralph McCallon, is now on exhibition at St Georges, Bermuda. Her hull, constructed from the waterline up on a concrete foundation, was designed by Cyril H Smith of Paget, Bermuda. I worked out her spars and rigging which had to reflect the fact that the rope, deadeyes, and blocks were salvaged from a large ship hence many items are not of the size that would have been chosen had the vessel been built under normal conditions.

A plan for a Dutch 'pinasschip' of the mid-seventeenth century – several are available – shows a vessel measuring 90ft from stem to stern with a breadth of 24ft and a depth of 12ft. Her single structural deck extends the full length without a break and she is pierced for seven guns on a side. The after forecastle bulkhead is about 22ft abaft the stem, the enclosed halfdeck space is about 30ft long, and the cabin on the halfdeck is about 17ft long. There is no sail plan but from the mast positions and number of deadeyes shown on the hull her rig very likely was the same as for the *Black Pynnes*.[7]

In 1674 we find another named pinnace, the guard-ship *Salvator Mundi* shown in a view of the Norwegian port of Trondheim. Her hull appears similar to that of the Dutch 'pinasschip' and her rig is the same as that of the *Black Pynnes* of nearly a century earlier. This date marks about the end of the use of the term 'pinnace' to designate a seagoing vessel. At the Restoration of Charles II of England in 1660, Samuel Pepys made a list of the vessels in the English navy but pinnaces were not identified as a type. The fighting ships were divided into six 'rates' depending on size and armament and buried in the list of '6th rates' was the old *Henrietta* of 1626, the only one of the group called a pinnace. Probably other small vessels occasionally called pinnaces were listed in one of the thirteen other classifications employed by Pepys.

Undoubtedly, vessels of hull types and rigs other than those discussed in detail were at one time or another called pinnaces. The material in this chapter, however, will suffice to illustrate a few of the possibilities and to indicate some of the complexities of marine research. As the seventeenth century progressed we find in American colonial records the increasing use of other type names to denote small vessels employed for the same purposes as pinnaces in the early part of the century. The term 'pinnace' gradually disappeared except as the name of the private pulling boat of the captain of a man-of-war.

CHAPTER 5

A Coastal Trader –
A Colonial Bark circa 1640

Scattered through the chronicles and records of seventeenth-century colonial America are repeated references to vessels called 'barks'. The spelling varies considerably – bark, barke, barque, and even barkque. Most perusers of this material immediately think of a vessel carrying the present day 'bark' rig ('barque' in the United Kingdom) which is basically three-masted although there have been four- and five-masted barks. The distinguishing feature of the present rig is that the aftermost mast carries fore-and-aft sails only while the others are square-rigged. Continuous employment of this three-masted rig since the fifteenth century is easy to trace; we have noted earlier that it was the basic 'ship' rig of the early seventeenth century. A reference to a small bark of 12 tons, however, rules out the possibility that such a rig was fitted on all seventeenth-century barks and that the term 'bark', in whatever spelling we choose, then defined a rig.

The English word 'bark', denoting a vessel and not a rig, is derived from the Latin *barca* via the same word in Italian and the French *barque*. Related vessels which will influence our final definition are the 'barcaza' of Cadiz and the 'barca longa' which was employed around the Iberian Peninsula. These two types were adopted by the French as the 'barcasse' and the 'barque longue'. In a few instances 'barca longa' and its variations in other languages seems to have been used as a sort of naval rating similar to sloop which usually was everything but sloop-rigged; 'Barkalongen' *Flyende Fisk* appeared far to the north in 1687 as one of a flotilla of Danish vessels.[1]

Two sources of information consulted in connection with the vessels in the previous chapters, Mainwaring and Boteler, are of no use in trying to define a bark as neither listed it in their books. In 1611, however, Randle Cotgrave translated the French *barque* into English as 'a barque, little ship, great boat'. The *New English Dictionary* notes that the word was taken from the French language into English in the sense of a small vessel with sails. The use of the term 'vessel' implies at least one deck while 'little ship' probably means that the standard ship rig of the early 1600s was carried, two masts square-rigged with a single lateen sail on the mizzenmast. 'Great boat', on the other hand, leads us to visualize a large open craft, very likely a double-ender; such a craft probably would have had only a two-masted rig.

The French dictionaries of Guillet, 1686, and Aubin, 1702, have nearly identical definitions which may be stated in English as:

> Barque – It is a vessel with one deck which has three masts, the main, the fore, and the mizzen; the largest are seldom of over one hundred tons. Some have a portable shelter aft which extends forward to the main mast.

As for the related 'barque longue', Guillet and Aubin said that it:

> . . . is a small undecked vessel, longer and shallower than ordinary barques, with a sharp bow, which is propelled by sails and oars. It has the form of a shallop and in some places is called a double-shallop.

In his *L'Architecture Navale* of 1677 Dassie gave the dimensions of a typical 'barque longue' – length from stem to stern 40ft, breadth 9ft, and depth 4½ft. Inasmuch as an ordinary barque was large enough to carry a three-masted rig it seems to me that the 'longer' and 'shallower' of Guillet and Aubin must have been referring to proportions rather than to absolute dimensions. Their statement can then be reworded so that for equal lengths, a more normal basis for comparing vessels, the 'barque longue' was narrower and shallower than an ordinary barque.

In describing the 'barcaza' ('barcasse') Lescallier used about the same wording in 1777 as Aubin in 1702. She was an undecked boat with a high stem and relatively sharp ends having a length of between 30ft and 40ft, a breadth of 8ft or 9ft, and a depth of about 5ft. Her rig was that of the Biscay shallop – large square mainsail and small square foresail – and she could be rowed with seven or more oars on a side. A 'barcaza' was considered an excellent sailer.

From valuation records of English privateersmen of 1590 we can infer that construction had some bearing on what constituted a seventeenth-century bark. Vessels in active service had been attached and the valuations, made in connection with suits against their owners, undoubtedly represented good current values for type and age.[2]

In January 1590 two ship carpenters and two ship masters appraised the 16-year old 'good shippe Katheryn of Waymouthe' of 35 tons burden. She carried the normal ship rig of the period; bonnets were listed for the fore- and mainsails but there was no spritsail. In April of the same year an appraisal was made of the 'good shippe or barkque called the Barque Waye', 45 tons burden and 7 years old, and 'a Certen Pinnace called the ffortunatus of London', 40 tons burden and 6 years old. The *Barque Way* also seems to have carried the basic ship rig, but she may have had pole masts instead of separate lower and top masts. Unfortunately for our pinnace study, neither sails nor spars were itemized for the *ffortunatus.* The comparative values were:

	Katheryn	Barque Way	ffortunatus
Age	16 years	7 years	6 years
Burden	35 tons	45 tons	40 tons
Value of hull, spars, rigging and sails	£62-10s	£29-0s	£34-12s
Value of hull	£50-0	£20-0	—
Value of spars	£2-0	£2-10	—
Value of rigging	£3-10	£2-0	—
Value of sails	£7-0	£4-10	—

From our earlier descriptions we can assume that as a ship the *Katheryn* would have had two decks in the main hull, a forecastle, and a poop. With the lowest valuations of the three vessels in spite of the greatest burden, the *Bark Way* probably had the simplest hull – one deck and a minimum of superstructures – hence we can conclude that hull configuration and construction and not rig determined the classification of a seventeenth-century bark. We should not conclude, however, that all barks were single-decked as reports of some expeditions indicate that the space needed for cargo, stores, and a vessel's company would have required two decks in the hull.

It is interesting to note that barks were not specifically mentioned in the Shipwrights' Charter of 1612 yet there are many references to them in records on both sides of the Atlantic. About 1620 the 'Book of Trade' of the Society of Merchant Venturers of Bristol, England, listed 'The names of such shippes & Barkes which with the marchandizes belonging to the marchants of Bristoll have bine taken & lost since the year 1610'. In 1626 the mayor of Bristol had a survey made of 'all the Shippes, barques, and vessels, now within or imployed at Sea'.[3] Governor William Bradford, in his journal *Of Plimoth Plantation*, referred to barks about twenty times and in the *History of New England* by John Winthrop, governor of the Massachusetts Bay colony, barks are mentioned on about thirty occasions.

THE MAYFLOWER

Among other references to barks by early New Englanders are those of Thomas Lechford in 1645 and Edward Johnson in 1650.[4] Lechford wrote that the colonists were building ships 'and had a good store of barks, catches, lighters, shallops, and other vessels' while Johnson noted that 'many a fair ship had her framing and finishing here, besides lesser vessels, barques and ketches'. It is interesting that neither Lechford nor Johnson mentioned pinnaces.

In a search through such source material, it is soon apparent that 'bark' was employed in two senses – in the general sense referring to vessels within a certain size range whether or not the exact type was known and in the specific sense to identify certain vessels. There were several instances where Bradford and Winthrop referred to ships, pinnaces, and even shallops as barks; other cases may be found in Hakluyt's *Voyages* as, for example, when a ship and a pinnace were called two barks. Bradford never mentioned the sizes of barks except to call one 'small' and another 'great', but those in Winthrop's *History* ranged from 12 to 50 tons. The records of the port of Boston for 1661–62 listed barks from 30 to 50 tons in size.[5] The *Foreign Correspondence* of the Connecticut Colony, 15 July 1680, mentioned two barks owned in the colony, one of 12 and the other of 30 tons.[6]

On the other hand, certain vessels were seldom if ever referred to except as barks thus establishing the fact that they were distinguished by one or a combination of features. On his second voyage in search of the Northwest Passage in 1577 Martin Frobisher had one ship, the *Aid* of 200 tons, and two barks, the *Gabriel* and *Michael* of about 30 tons each. In Hakluyt's account these vessels are consistently referred to by type. Another in this category was the 30-ton *Blessing of the Bay*, built for Governor Winthrop on the Mystic River at what is now Medford, Massachusetts, and launched on 4 July 1631. Winthrop made an even more specific reference to another bark, the 25-ton 'Norsey' (North Sea) bark that arrived at Boston on 28 November 1635. From this we may infer that a North Sea bark had some feature to distinguish it from other barks.[7]

A few of Bradford's specific references to barks are worthy of note. Concerning the trading activities of one Edward Ashley in 1629 he wrote, referring to the merchant backers in England:[8]

> They were forct to buy him a barque allso, and to furnish her with a mr. & men, to transporte his corne & provissions (of which he put of much); for ye Indeans of those parts have no corne growing, and at harvest, after corne is ready, ye weather grows foule and ye seas dangerous, so as he could doe litle good with his shallope for yt purposs.

A COLONIAL BARK

Here was a trading venture that had been carried on with an open shallop but experience showed that a decked vessel was needed for protection of the cargo and its own safety. The vessel provided was called a bark although Bradford had mentioned pinnaces in connection with other operations. In other examples he noted the loading of a house frame into the hold of a 'greate new barke' and the sale of items including 'housing, boats, bark, and all implements belonging to ye same'. The latter was a definite differentiation between the small open shallops and a larger decked vessel.

Governor Winthrop had several specific items regarding barks in addition to those previously mentioned. There was the bark *Warwick* that was engaged in coastwise trading between 1630 and 1632, one item referring to the carriage of corn from Virginia to various northern settlements. In 1631 he noted the following:[9]

> A small bark of Salem, of about twelve tons, coming toward the bay, John Elston and two of Mr Cradock's fishermen being in her, and two tons of stone, and three hogheads of train oil, was overset in a gust, and, being buoyed up by the oil, she floated up and down forty-eight hours, and the three men sitting upon her, till Henry Way his boat, coming by, espied them and saved them.

The fact that when the craft capsized the cargo of oil was trapped and provided buoyancy is a good indication that this bark was decked.

During a great storm, probably a hurricane, on 16 August 1635:[10]

> . . . a bark of Mr Allerton's was cast away upon Cape Ann, and twenty-one persons drowned. . . None were saved but one Mr Thacher and his wife. . . The man was cast on shore when he had been (as he thought) a quarter of an hour beaten up and down by the waves, not being able to swim one stroke; and his wife sitting in the scuttle of the bark, the deck was broke off, and was brought on shore, as she stuck on it.

The present Thacher's Island was named after these survivors of the disaster.

In spite of all this background it is obvious that we still cannot say that a bark must have certain features and that any deviation would require a different classification. The possibilities, however, are fewer than in the case of the pinnace. Figs 23, 24, and 25 show my ideas on the form, arrangement, construction, and rig of a New England-built bark of about 1640 intended for coastwise trading and fishing. This bark is small even by the standards of the smaller New England coasting schooners of the late nineteenth century. By the tonnage rule given in the first chapter she measures practically 29 tons which puts her about in the middle of Winthrop's size range.

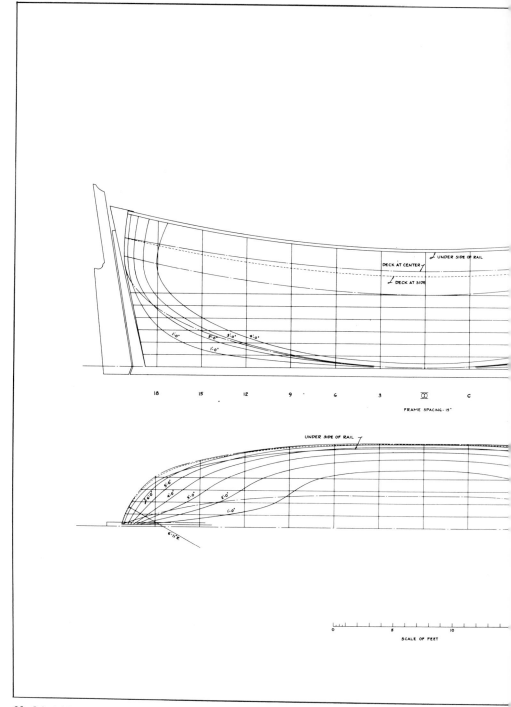

23. *Colonial Bark c1640 – Lines*

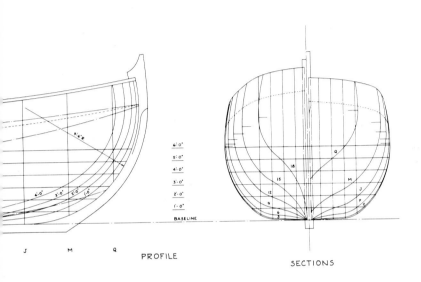

PROFILE

SECTIONS

NOTE - LINES ARE DRAWN TO INSIDE OF PLANKING

LENGTH ON THE KEEL	35'- 0"
BREADTH TO INSIDE OF PLANK	13'- 9"
DEPTH - TOP OF KEEL TO THE BREADTH	6'- 0"
BURDEN - TONS	29

WATERLINES

A
COLONIAL BARK
ca. 1640

William A. Baker
NAVAL ARCHITECT
HINGHAM   MASS.

PLATE I - LINES

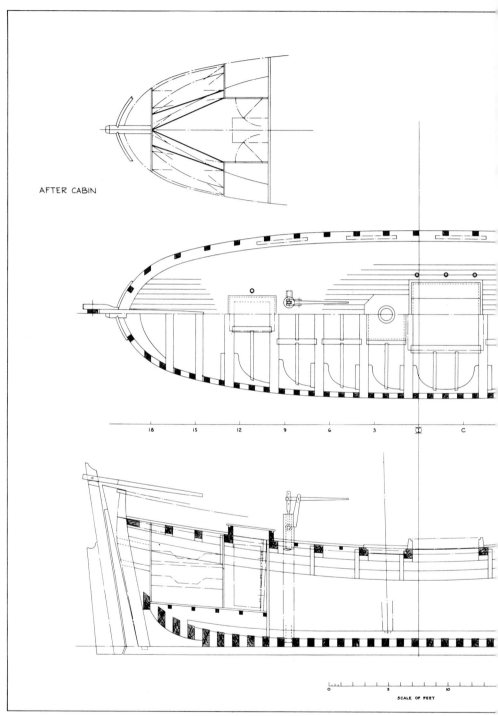

AFTER CABIN

18   15   12   9   6   3   C

SCALE OF FEET
0   5   10

24. *Colonial Bark c1640 – Arrangement & Construction*

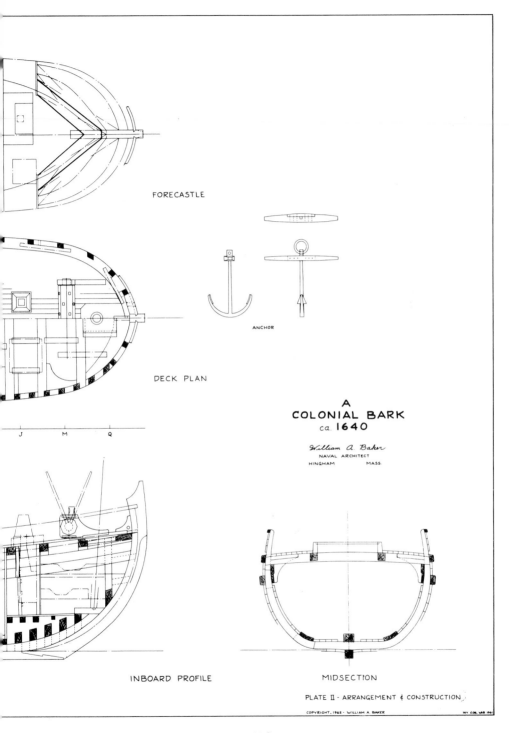

FORECASTLE

DECK PLAN

ANCHOR

J   M   Q

**A
COLONIAL BARK**
ca. **1640**

William A. Baker
NAVAL ARCHITECT
HINGHAM   MASS.

INBOARD PROFILE

MIDSECTION

PLATE II - ARRANGEMENT & CONSTRUCTION

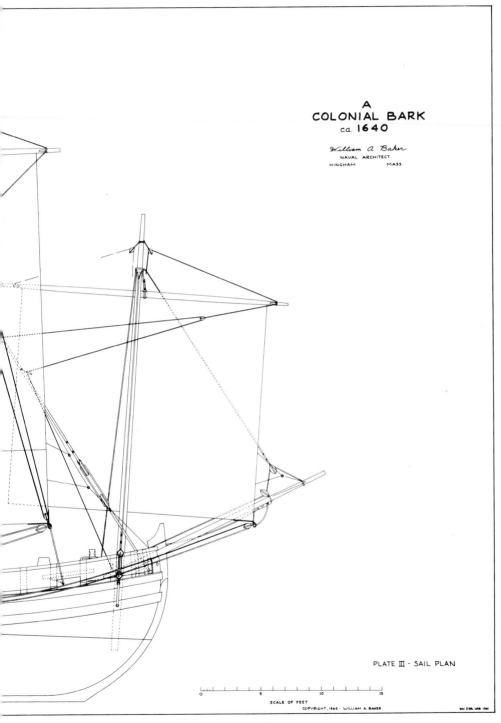

105

THE MAYFLOWER

As must be apparent from the material available on any of the types of vessels discussed so far, such a re-creation is the sum of a few known facts, some reasonable assumptions based on later vessels, and a professional judgment. I would not want to say that she represents any named vessels even though Winthrop's *Blessing of the Bay* was called a 30-ton bark. Bradford's 'greate new barke' may have been about the same size. She could not have been much larger and still been able to sail up the Connecticut River to Windsor with the house frame and other cargo, for early reports gave only a fathom of water over the bar at the mouth of the river at Saybrook.

The hull form depicted in Fig 23 is in the tradition of a 'great boat' rather than a 'small ship', a double-ender in the true line of descent from the old boats of northern Europe, similar to an enlarged shallop. This is justified by a 1671 court case that involved a 'Deck Shallop or barque'.[11] The hull sections were drawn by the sweep method although such a hull might have been whole-molded. The outline of the midship bend was delineated by three arcs; in drawing the sections forward and aft the center for the body sweep always remained on the centerline.

The arrangement and construction of the re-created bark were considered together as in many instances the requirements of one dictated the details of the other; from both points of view this new bark is about as simple as possible. As a vessel intended for trading and fishing her hold is spacious and there are low bulwarks all around to help keep the crew on deck when fishing. Trading vessels of about the size of our bark are known to have been handled by three men and a boy but the standard crew of similar Breton and Cornish fishing craft was six men and a boy. To provide for the possibility of carrying a few passengers – the sea was the only convenient means of travel between most of the North American settlements – our bark has eight crude bunks. The accommodations are shown equally divided forward and aft and separated from the cargo space by bulkheads but neither may be fully justified. Both the 'forecastle', to use the time honored name for the crew's quarters, and the after cabin are at best but damp dark holes. The forecastle would also be smoky, for it contains a simple brick fireplace for cooking. In addition to the bunks aft there are two lockers for spare gear. The deck running flush from bow to stern makes the forecastle and after cabin a little more cramped than might be absolutely necessary. A small rise in the deck at bow and stern would have been quite reasonable but would have destroyed the basic simplicity of the craft.

106

A COLONIAL BARK

Let us look at the main features of our bark starting with the foremast, a 7¾in diameter spar stepped close to the stem. Next comes a simple log windlass which is pawled by its handspikes to the deck. Just abaft it to starboard is the hatch to the forecastle while to port is a clay-lined wooden chimney for the fireplace. This chimney is portable and can be replaced in bad weather by a hatch cover fitted to the low coaming. Nearby would be a water cask lashed to ringbolts in the deck.

The main cargo hatch is just forward of the 11½in diameter mainmast. It is closed by four boards and made tight against the sea and weather by a tarpaulin or two; ringbolts are provided on each side for passing securing lashings. A single log pump is located near the after end of the cargo hold. A small hatch on the centerline gives access to the after quarters and the stores lockers. From the hatch to the stern the deck is unobstructed to allow room for working the tiller. A shelter might be provided over this area in the form of a wooden framework on which a tarpaulin could be stretched.

A few items in the miscellaneous category complete the bark's normal equipment. There are a few heavy horizontal timbers (kevels) plus several cleats secured to the inside of the bulwark stanchions for the belaying of running rigging. Stowed forward are two 350lb anchors; their hemp cables are 7in in circumference. Three or four heavy sweeps about 20ft long, usually stowed along the bulwarks, will be found handy in calm spells or for moving the bark around a harbor. These sweeps will work against single 2in diameter thole pins set in blocks fixed to the inside of the bulwark, port and starboard, in clear spaces forward of and abaft the mainmast; grommets secure the sweeps to the pins. Our bark is large enough to need some sort of a small boat. The most common and cheapest of the small craft in the New England colonies was the dugout log canoe; one can easily be carried on deck or towed astern.

As for the actual construction of the bark, the details shown in Fig 24 would have been well known to a shipwright of the 1640s and there would have been no need to set them down in graphic form. The sizes of the various structural members were derived from seventeenth-century scantling tables and confirmed by specifications and wrecks of the period. As in the mother country oak and pine were the usual shipbuilding materials in old New England. The natural knees were probably of oak but the qualities of the native larch, hackmatack to the Indians, undoubtedly were discovered early. Locust, a very durable wood, was plentiful in the seventeenth century; it is said that

Winthrop's *Blessing of the Bay* was constructed entirely of this species.

The first really productive iron works in the English North American colonies was operated at Hammersmith, now Saugus, Massachusetts, from about 1646 to 1675. In view of this, it is undoubtedly true that all the iron used in earlier days was brought from England, probably in rough bar form from which the local smiths could forge the necessary pins, bolts, and other ironwork. As iron was relatively scarce even at home, wooden pins – treenails – were commonly employed for fastening all heavy timbers. Nails were used in thin planking, say under 1¼in thick, where treenails would not hold.

If the hull of the bark were to be completed today some thought would be given to the painting of it. Such a thought probably would not have troubled anyone in the seventeenth century, certainly not in the colonies, for paint as we know it was not then used as a protective coating. As noted in connection with the *Mayflower II* the topsides might have been coated with Stockholm tar and the wales and rails picked out with black, an earth red, or a similar yellow. If the under-body received any coating it was more likely pitch than the white lead, tallow, and sulfur mixture mentioned earlier.

In rigging the bark the first move would be to step the two masts noted in connection with her arrangement. In view of the earlier material indicating that barks had *three* masts it is reasonable and proper for the reader to ask, why only two? The several sound reasons supporting my belief that small barks had a two-masted square rig follow.

As we have noted that 'bark' was taken from French into English in the sense of a small vessel with sails let us look to France for portraits of seventeenth-century 'barques'. Jean Baptiste Colbert, the powerful minister who did so much for the French marine during the second half of the seventeenth century, left a valuable collection of papers pertaining to ships and shipping. Among them is a series of drawings, acquired by Colbert in 1679, depicting the types of ships, vessels, and small craft employed in the various regions of France. Because of the slowness of change in things marine as shown by other data, it is not unreasonable to consider that the types of small vessels shown had been in use for at least the previous forty years.

The first portrait that we will look at, from a sheet showing vessels of Bayonne, may have been what Cotgrave had in mind when he gave his alternate definition of a bark as 'a great boat'. As may be seen in

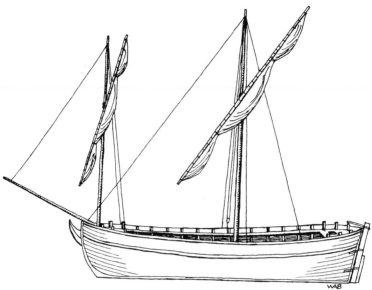

26. Barque of Bayonne – after Colbert, Dessein . . . de Vaisseau

Fig 26 she was a double-ender about 43ft in length over all with a depth of about 5ft to the rail. The caption on the original sheet noted that there were many similar barques ranging in size from 12 to 60 tons which traded to Rochelle, Bordeaux, Nantes, and other ports. The crew of such a barque has five or six men.

This barque of Bayone had a short deck at each end connected by a gangway along each side leaving the cargo space entirely open. She was rigged with two masts each of which carried a single square sail, the foresail being larger than normal for the Biscay shallop rig. The presence of a bowsprit indicates that this foresail could have been carried when sailing to windward. Apparently the yards were shown in the diagonal positions for the artist's convenience so as not to interfere with other objects. Etchings of similar craft show, however, that this was the normal position, presumably to cut down windage, when they were being propelled by oars. The size of the crew of this barque indicates that oars must have been used at times.

A second French barque is sketched in Fig 27. She was from Bordeaux where similar vessels ranged from 15 to 50 tons in size; her normal crew was three men and a boy. This barque is definitely a decked vessel with a square stern. In this she departs from the 'great boat' concept yet she is far from being a 'small ship' as there are no superstructures, just a small rise in the deck aft to provide a little more

27. *Barque of Bordeaux – after Colbert,* Dessein . . . de Vaisseau

room in the stern cabin. Her length over all was about 55ft with a depth of about 8ft to the deck at side. This Bordeaux vessel also had a two-masted square rig but, unlike that of the barque from Bayonne, it had the proportions of the Biscay shallop rig. No bowsprit was shown but the Bordeaux craft may have employed a spar bowline on the foresail when beating to windward. It is interesting to note that these two barques are from the period when Guillet's definition called for three masts.

An English bark of about a century earlier than these French examples and similar to the one from Bordeaux is shown in Fig 28. She was the 60-ton *Isaac* of London which was depicted on a map of Ireland's Smerwick Bay drawn in 1580. While her foresail is about the same size as her main she could carry a main topsail set flying, thus preserving the proportions of the Biscay shallop rig. As well as being classed as a pinnace because of her use the vessel shown in Fig 15 might also have been called a bark.

A COLONIAL BARK

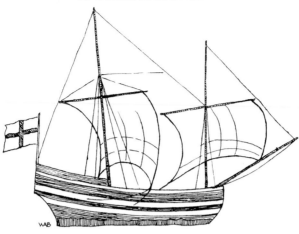

28. *Bark* Isaac *of London c1580*

A painting by Pieter de Zeelander, a seventeenth-century artist, of vessels sailing off the coast of the Netherlands includes a small two-master, sketched in Fig 29, which is flying an ensign bearing the English Cross of St George. She is about the size of our colonial bark but seems to have a square stern with perhaps a small cabin aft; a number of late seventeenth-century New England-built barks also had square sterns. Unlike our bark this small English vessel has a main topmast on which a topsail could be set flying.

Pictorial representations of colonial North American vessels are scarce. Those that are available, even well into the mid-1700s, must be viewed with caution. The sketching of a North American city or other view on the spot with the final engraving being done in England or on the Continent seems to have been the standard practice. When vessels were required to fill an expanse of waterfront the engraver often copied some from available prints; in many cases it is possible to identify the sources of the vessels shown.

The first woodcut map known to have been cut within the bounds of the present United States appeared in 1677. It is thought to be the work of Boston printer John Foster as an illustration for the Reverend William Hubbard's story of King Philip's War, *A Narrative of the Trouble with the Indians in New England*, which Foster printed. This woodcut shows a bird's eye view of part of the present New England as seen from a point well at sea off Cape Cod. The Connecticut coastline extends west along the left hand margin to a little beyond New Haven; in the lower right hand corner the coast of Maine is carried just beyond Pemaquid. Among the various decorative features are five vessels under sail, all properly drawn with respect to a north-westerly wind.[12]

Two of these vessels are ships shown from the port quarter as they sail south-west into Massachusetts Bay on the starboard tack. Both have the usual three masts and carry, in addition to a lateen sail, a square topsail on their mizzenmasts. One has topgallant sails on her fore and main masts but neither carries a square spritsail under her bowsprit. A third sizeable vessel is shown from the starboard bow on the port tack headed north-east out of Massachusetts Bay. She carries what in the latter part of the seventeenth century was called the ketch rig; this will be discussed in the next chapter. The fourth vessel, a small one, is well inshore off the mouth of the Piscataqua River heading northerly close hauled on the port tack. She carries the same rig as the *Pilgrim Shallop II* and the pinnace *Virginia*, a sprit mainsail and a single staysail.

29. *English bark c1650 – after Pieter de Zeelander*

A COLONIAL BARK

Of primary interest to us is the fifth vessel sketched in Fig 30 which I believe is intended to represent a colonial bark. Shown from the star-board bow on the port tack she apparently is a two-masted square-rigger, similar in many respects to the *Isaac*, Fig 28. The mainmast of the Foster vessel carries a topsail but I do not believe that one could be set on her foremast; here again we have the basic proportions of the Biscay shallop rig.

30. *Two-masted vessel – after Foster*

What we do not know, of course, is the source of these vessels. We do not know whether John Foster was responsible for the entire map and art work or whether he cut the block from another's drawing. In either case there remains the question of whether the vessels were derived from some other print or were based on local knowledge. Considering the way the five vessels are carefully shown sailing to the same wind, a condition that does not apply on many other maps, it is unlikely that they were copied from any European print. I believe that they represent actual types of vessels to be seen in New England waters in 1677.

Considering that many New England shallops carried two-masted square rigs the previously mentioned 1671 court case involving a

'Deck Shallop or barque' implies the same rig on colonial barks. The final proof, however, for the two-masted rig on our bark depends on the definition of another type of vessel. This is the 'snow' whose early history is as confused as that of any type. In English the type name, related to the French *senau* and the Dutch *snauw*, can be traced back to 1676 but its use did not become widespread for another half century or so.

There is no doubt but that the vessel normally considered to be a seagoing snow was a two-masted square-rigger that has been of interest to those who classify vessels by rig because of a peculiarity in masting. It and the final form of the brig were almost indistinguishable – in fact, many of the late vessels classed as brigs were, technically speaking, actually snows. The brig carried both a square and a fore-and-aft sail on the main lower mast while the fore-and-aft sail on a snow was set on a separate mast located a foot or so abaft the mainmast. This additional spar was of small diameter and was stepped on deck; its head was supported by the main top.

Aubin gave two definitions for senaus. One definitely sailed on inland waters but the other was a seagoing vessel:

> It is a *barque longue* employed by the Flemish for privateering. She carries twenty-five men at the most.

Here we are back to the 'barque longue' which implies the basic two-masted square rig of the Biscay shallop.

Turning to New England records the 'Snow or Barke Sea flower . . . a Pinke Sternd Vessell . . . of about Twenty Tuns' was built in 1709 at Newbury at the mouth of the Merrimac River.[13] Here we have a most interesting vessel. The 'pinke stern' means of course a double-ender in line with Cotgrave's 'great boat' definition while the use of the word 'snow' indicates a two-masted square rig either via Aubin's definition or the commonly accepted later one of the rig classifiers. The uncertainty expressed by the use of 'Snow or Barke' implies that the year 1709 was in the transition period between the use of the old type designation of bark and the full employment of the newly fashionable name 'snow'.

Here is a note indicating that 'snow' originally may have defined a hull form rather than a rig:[14]

> The old Dutch word *snau*, *snauu*, *snauw*, etc has the same meaning as the present low-German word *Schnautze*, ie *snout*. Richey says in his *Hamburgisches Indioticon*, 1775, p272: 'Ships to go easier and quicker are built

114

A COLONIAL BARK

"op de snau", ie they are not round at the bow, like transport ships, but sharp and thin like frigates, yachts, etc.' This suggests that the snow was originally named for its shape, and that the rig was a later feature. In favour of this is a remark of 1789, to be found in Kluge's *Seemannsprache*, 1911, p698: 'It was well known that the biggest ship might be as good a sailer if it was well constructed like a snow from underneath (wenn's gut gebauet wäre als eine Schnaue von untern).'

XVII. *Model of Colonial bark c1640, by E A R Ronnberg, Jr.* (Author)

THE MAYFLOWER

Going a step beyond our little 1640 bark to round out the rig development, let us return briefly to the *Barque Way* and also consider a Dutch engraving of about 1700. We have noted that the normal Biscay shallop with a big square mainsail and small square foresail did not set the latter when beating to windward and the craft handled well enough under the mainsail alone. When, however, arrangements were made to carry the foresail when beating, either by adding a bowsprit to which the fore bowlines could be led or employing a spar bowline as shown in Fig 16, the rig could have been somewhat unbalanced. The additional sail forward, tending to hold the vessel's head off the wind, might have required considerable lee helm to keep her on course but there were two obvious solutions to this problem.

The simplest solution would likely have been the addition of balancing sail area aft, a third mast with a small lateen sail. Such an addition may have accounted for the three masts on the *Barque Way*. The comparative values given earlier in this chapter indicate that she had the simple hull required by the dictionary definitions but, with the three-masted rig, the appraisers may have felt that they should dignify her a little hence used the word 'shippe' too. Several portraits of small vessels with simple hulls, both round and square sterned, can be cited but an interesting example that illustrates this solution is sketched in Fig 31.

31. *Scottish coal cat – after A van der Laan from S van der Meulen*

A COLONIAL BARK

Called by the artist a 'Scottish coal cat' she is considered to represent a well developed type of North Sea cargo carrier of the late seventeenth century. Perhaps Winthrop's 25-ton 'Norsey' bark of 1635 mentioned earlier was of this type. In many ways the vessel sketched looks Dutch but this is not surprising in view of the widespread Dutch influence in maritime matters following the Anglo-Dutch Wars. With her double-ended hull this 'coal cat' is following the tradition of the 'great boat'. She has a raised quarter deck aft to give more room in the stern cabin and, in keeping with the definition of a bark, there is a small shelter over the after part of this deck. The galley stack forward shows the location of the crew's quarters under a raised forecastle deck.

This cat's mainmast is a substantial spar with a light topmast but no top or crosstrees. Apparently the topsail was set flying; a detailed portrait of an earlier vessel with a similar rig shows topsail bowlines secured to the lower masthead ready to be hitched to the sail when it was sent aloft. The foremast and its single square sail are quite small and bear the Biscay shallop rig proportions to the main. The short mizzenmast is stepped well aft. The standing rigging shown is about the absolute minimum. The mainmast has three shrouds on a side and a stay leading to the foremast at the deck; the topmast is completely unsupported. The foremast has but one shroud on each side as does the mizzen which also has a stay leading to the mainmast at the deck. No bowsprit is shown but it may have been rigged in while the cat was in the harbor or else a spar bowline was used on the foresail instead of regular bowlines. A rather surprising item of the rig is the relatively large main staysail.

The second solution to the unbalance of the Biscay shallop rig when means were available for carrying the foresail on all points of sailing required that both masts, hence the center of effort of the whole sail plan, be shifted aft. This I believe was the course followed in the development of the later barks and ultimately the snow. The bark on John Foster's map, Fig 30, seems to have her masts further aft than we would expect from the French examples in Colbert's collection.

The unbalanced rig, however, was not as serious as it might seem at first to one accustomed to handling a modern short-keeled racing yacht. The helm response of a cruising yacht with a similar keel configuration would quickly wear out her crew. Cruising yachts usually have relatively long keels and here it can be noted that a vessel with a long keel can tolerate a considerable shift in the center of effort of the sails without becoming unmanageable. Hence, for our long-

THE MAYFLOWER

keeled little bark, we have retained the large main and small fore of the original Biscay shallop sail plan.

The various items of rigging shown in Fig 25 follow seventeenth-century practice as shown by engravings, etchings, and paintings of similar vessels and as described in Dr R C Anderson's book *Seventeenth-Century Rigging* (London, 1955). The sizes of the rigging are:

		Circ. Main (inches)	Circ. Fore (inches)
Shrouds		4	2¾
Stays		6	3¾
	collar	5½	—
	runner	—	2¾
Parrels		3	2¼
Halyard—	tie	5	4
	purchase	2¾	2¾
Braces—	pendants	2¾	2
	falls	2¼	1½
Lifts		2¾	2
Sheets		3	2¼
Tacks		3¾	3
Clewlines		2	—
Bowlines—	bridles	2	1½
	falls	2¼	2

With the rigging completed and sails bent to their yards the bark will be ready to carry corn north to the Indians, to transport a house frame south around Cape Cod and up the Connecticut River, or to go fishing to the eastward. We can hope that her crew will not have to spend forty-eight hours on her side, bobbing up and down, because they let her overset in a gust.

CHAPTER 6

The Colonial Ketch

The ketch or 'catch', to use the early seventeenth century spelling, was introduced to the New England scene by Governor Bradford of Plymouth when he noted in his journal in 1624:[1]

> The ship-carpenter that was sent them, was an honest and very industrious man, and followed his labour very dilligently, and made all that were imployed with him doe ye like; he quickly builte them 2 very good & strong shalops (which after did them grate service), and a great and strong lighter, and had hewne timber for 2 catches. . .

The colony never did get these two catches, for the ship-carpenter 'fell into a feaver in ye hote season of ye year, and though he had the best means ye place coulde aforde, yet he dyed' and there was no other carpenter capable of utilizing the hewn timber to complete the vessels. Why the decision to construct two catches, the instruction from Robert Cushman, the colony's agent in England, instead of two barks or pinnaces, which were mentioned so often in the early records, is an intriguing problem for marine researchers.

Following this introduction there are indications of the increasing use of ketches in the maritime activities of the New England colonies. The above quotation is Bradford's only reference to the type. Winthrop mentioned ketches seven times in his *History of New England* and from our references in the previous chapter we can note that both Lechford in 1645 and Johnson in 1650 listed ketches. In 1680 the estate of merchant John Turner of Salem included part or full ownership of nine ketches, one pink, one ship, one shallop, one sloop, and one pleasure boat. By 1697 there were sixty fishing ketches sailing out of Salem alone.[2]

The story of the ketch is confused, for the name was used for a special type of naval vessel, for yachts, and for certain merchant vessels. The type name has come down to us as defining a two-masted square-rigged vessel that is usually described as a ship without a fore-mast. A typical vessel carrying this rig is sketched in Fig 32. This definition implies that the naval vessel, usually called a bomb-ketch in England, the yacht, and the merchant ketch of the seventeenth century were rigged in the same manner. This is true to a certain extent, particularly toward the end of the century. The bomb-ketch and the yacht version were relatively latecomers in the ketch story and, in the early stages of their development, there probably was little to differentiate them from the widely employed merchant version. With the passing of time, features peculiar to their special employment were adopted; it is obvious that a royal yacht would have differed greatly from a grubby cargo carrier.

32. *Bomb-ketch, 1695 – after Chatterton,* Sailing Ships and Their Story

Some of the confusion and lack of definite information concerning ketches may stem from the state of English marine art prior to the eighteenth century. Researchers investigating the development of British fishing boats and coastal craft have found little to define off-shore vessels before 1700 and even less for inshore craft. It is difficult to determine from the few available representations of small boats whether they are fishing boats or ships' boats. Starting in the Middle Ages and carrying on into later periods, these familiar objects rarely attracted artists. There is no known painting of an English fishing boat by an English artist before the seventeenth century. As ketches and presumably other small craft were employed for trading as well as fishing, the same probably can be said for small trading vessels.[3]

During the first three-quarters of the seventeenth century there was little marine art that could be called English; the majority of the existing portrayals of English vessels are by Dutch artists who were brought to England or otherwise commissioned to depict certain battles or other events. In 1674, by the royal order of Charles II, the Willem van de Veldes, father and son, became for all practical purposes the official marine artists of England. Each was paid one hundred pounds a year, the father 'for taking and making draughts of sea fights' and the son 'for putting the said draughts into colours'. In view of these appointments, it is natural to find that the English vessels portrayed by the van de Veldes were mainly the naval vessels and the new royal yachts. The van de Veldes had their own small vessel in which they accompanied the fleet into action and 'in taking and making draughts of sea fights' they were occasionally caught in the cross fire of opposing forces.

Yachts and yachting in the present sense were unknown in England before 1660 when the yacht *Mary* was presented to Charles II by the city of Amsterdam. The *Mary* and the other early yachts were not, however, ketches; they were finely decorated vessels having relatively high transom sterns and they carried a single-masted rig consisting of a fore-and-aft mainsail, one or two triangular headsails, and a square topsail. The ketch yachts came later but at least as early as 1682.

The van de Veldes do not seem to have produced identifiable pictures of the common British merchant vessels and by the time British artists turned to local scenes the normal small seventeenth-century vessels had developed into a variety of regional types that had acquired new names. Information on merchant ketches is so scarce that when the version is mentioned it is the later and larger version that comes to mind. It is absurd, however, to assume that the ketches that made up a large part of the late seventeenth-century New England fishing fleet or were employed in coastal trading were rigged like the complicated naval bomb-ketch.

Following the procedure of the previous chapters we will try to define by means of dictionaries and other descriptions what a seventeenth-century New England colonist may have meant by the term 'ketch'. Cotgrave in 1611 did not list the ketch in any of the recognized spellings; if the French then employed the type it was under some other name. Mainwaring assumed that his readers were familiar with London's fish market at Billingsgate: 'A ketch is a small boat such as useth to come to Billingsgate with mackerel, oysters, etc.' He further noted, 'We all call small vessels as ketches, hoyes, crays and the like, *small craft. . .*' In 1634 Boteler stated, 'As for ketches, they are smaller vessels than hoys, and yet so moulded and builte that they will endure and live (as the sea phrase is) in any sea whatsoever; and are withal of very good sail, and in that respect are very proper to wait upon great ships upon the service forementioned'.

One of the earliest uses of the type name in any of its recognized English forms was recorded in the Howard Household Books, 1481–1490, 397. In 1481 John Lord Howard was fitting out a squadron at Harwich on the east coast of England for service against the Scots. While at Harwich he employed two local 'caches', one for an unknown errand from Harwich to Manningtree, a simple trip up the River Stour, and the other to transport an unknown quantity of perishable cargoes, red ocher and hops – 'Rede oker to send be water with the sayd hoppes in Ferdes cache of Brekemlynsey'.[4] This indicates with little question that by 1481 a 'cache' was a decked vessel and that such vessels were in general use and readily available on the estuaries and rivers of south-eastern England. As Brekemlynsey was an early name for the modern Brightlingsea on the River Colne, some twenty-five miles or so around the coast from Harwich, this statement also implied a handy seaworthy vessel capable of dodging in and out of the many channels through the treacherous sand bars off that coast.

Chronologically, our next reference concerns a ketch on the River Thames in 1536: 'The same catche beying under sail in the reach over against Lymehouse.'[5] In 1561 we find that ketches were employed for fishing: 'Fyshermen that go a trawling for fyshe in catches or mongers.'[4] Coupled with the 1612 Shipwrights' Charter mentioned in the Introduction in which crayers were listed before ketches, a reference of 1580 indicates that size may have had something to do with type classifications: 'a small catch or craer of Sir William Wynters.'[4] The term 'craer', sometimes spelled 'craier' but usually 'crayer', simply meant 'carrier' and is by origin the same word.[6] Another indication of size was given by Captain John Smith in 1607: 'The river . . . is navigable . . . with catches and small barks 30 to 40 myles further.'[4] From the previous chapter we know that colonial barks ranged in size from twelve to sixty tons.

The handiness of a ketch implied by the 1481 employment along the coast was definitely stated in 1625: 'Catches, being short and round built, be verie apt to turne up and downe, and useful to goe to and fro, and to carry messages between shipp and shipp almost with any wind.'[7]

We might note at this point that one variation of the type name, 'catch', has the old meaning of 'chase' or 'pursuit' hence was a parallel to the Dutch 'jagt' that gave us our present 'yacht' which implies speed.[8] But what were the early ketches pursuing when they were carrying ocher and hops, mackerel and oysters? Perhaps the spelling 'cache' in the 1481 reference, at a time when many vessels were not decked, indicated a derivation from the French in the sense of a hole, a hiding place, a place to stow. It has been suggested that the name came from an old Italian word meaning 'tub' which might be an apt description of a craft that was 'short and round built'.[9]

With the foregoing definitions and descriptions as a background we can carry on and set down some conclusions concerning colonial-built ketches. Even from the earliest record of a 'cache' in 1481 which carried perishable cargoes there can be no doubt that the type was decked and not open. This conclusion is implied by other quoted items and specified in material to follow.

Ketches were small until late in the seventeenth century. Again this is implied and stated in the foregoing items. Just how small the English ketches were can be found in a manuscript of 1588 that gives the tonnage of several hired for various purposes. The *Ann* of Stroude measured 12 tons, the *Primrose* of the same port was of 20 tons, the *Bess* of Packlesom – the present Paglesham – was a 17-ton vessel, and an unnamed ketch from ffeversham measured 18 tons. There was also a ketch of 20 tons while the largest listed was a 30-tonner.[10] The ports mentioned are located on rivers flowing into the Thames estuary, the general region where the earliest ketches were found.

By 1588, however, some ketches were large enough to go to sea, at least within the English Channel. One was attached to the fleet that sailed from Chatham to Plymouth to meet the Spanish Armada while another was with the fleet that was watching the actions of the Duke of Parma, the Spanish commander in the Low Countries. The sizes of these ketches were not given but each had a crew of twelve which would be suitable for a burden of about thirty tons. In 1595 some ketches really did go to sea as two were with the Drake–Hawkins fleet that sailed to the Spanish Main.[11]

It would be of interest if some indication could be found of the size of the ketches for which the fever-stricken carpenter had hewn timbers at Plymouth in New England in 1624. The earliest colonial-built ketch for which a size was given was a 40-tonner mentioned by Winthrop in 1640; his six other references to the type do not give tonnages. The Boston Port Records for 1661–1662 list ketches ranging from 16 to 30 tons to compare with the 30 to 50 tons barks from the same source mentioned in the previous chapter. The tonnages of sixty ketches built in New England between 1676 and 1702 ranged from 12 to 80 tons; the latter was unusual as the next largest measured only 45 tons. Fifty-five of these ketches measured between 20 and 40 tons with the average being about 30 tons.[12]

From the 1625 description, Boteler's statements, and our knowledge of other small vessels of the period we can infer that a ketch was a stoutly-built double-ender. I believe that hull form and certain constructional features were important in defining a ketch. A statement in support of this concerned a Dutch prize of perhaps the early 1700s. Having a length of 36ft 4in, a breadth of 17ft, and a depth of hold of 4ft 9in, she was described as a 'round-stern ketch-built schuyt'.[13]

One constructional feature of a ketch apparently was that her deck be flush. This is in keeping with the 'endure and live in any sea' statement as superstructures could be a source of weakness. Small rises or falls, however, seem to have been acceptable. The following comments pertain to the flush deck requirement:[14]

> On June 22nd, 1682, the Navy Board was ordered to make a suit of sails for the new yacht building at Greenwich out of the canvas in store at Deptford. This must have been the *Fubbs*, and the reference might be worth following up, for she was undoubtedly ketch-rigged as will be seen from a Navy Board letter of November 1st, 1682. In this they sent 'an estimate of the charges of altering the *Isabella* yacht and making her fit for a ketch like the *Fubbs*'. The estimate is for £608.12s.0d., a large sum to be spent on altering a small new vessel of 52 tons. It was proposed not only to re-rig her, but virtually to rebuild her hull above water in order to make her flush-decked, as apparently a ketch ought to be. Clearly the Admiralty did not like the estimate, for on December 23rd, 1682, they instructed the Navy Board to 'make a contract with Sir Phineas Pett for building a new yacht at Greenwich with a flush deck, according to the dimensions etc of the enclosed agreement; and to present an estimate of the charge.' . . . This was the new *Isabella*, of 114 tons, and there can be little doubt that she was made a ketch. [This is confirmed by a sketch showing the locations of the main brace, sheet, and tack.]

XVIII. *The* Adventure *under sail, April 1970.* (Author)

THE MAYFLOWER

Court records have provided the details of two ketches built in Massachusetts, one in 1666 and the other in 1678. The first of these and the larger, built at Boston:[15]

> . . . was to be forty-four feet by the keel upon a straight line, two bee seventeen feet by the midship beam and two bee nearest nine feet deep in hold from plank to plank; she was also to have a pink stern and a close steerage and a fall into the hold under the half deck and two bee strong stinch and thith with all other conveniences as such vessels have when they go off the stocks . . .

The 1678 ketch, built by William Carr of Salisbury, also had a pink stern and was:[16]

> . . . to bee in lenght by ye keele thirty fower feet, in breadth twelve foot by ye beame & six foot deep in ye hold to bee every way shipshapen. The said ketch to be built with two inch white oake planke to ye upp wale, & with inch & halfe white oake plank upward, & to be seiled fore & aft with ye like condicond two inch planke: To lay her deck with good two inch pine plank: the fore castle to be raised twelve Inches & ye cabin abaft to be raisd two foot, with scuttles & hatches sutable. . .

In addition to this evidence for double-ended ketches in New England, 53 of the 60 ketches built between 1676 and 1702 also were double-enders. The other 7 had square sterns, the earliest of these being built in 1694.

Ketches were handy vessels. Handiness obviously is not a quality imparted by construction. It is influenced to a certain extent by form, but it is directly affected by rig hence we must now face this complicated subject. The basic medieval rig for all sizes of vessels and a common rig for small craft through the seventeenth century was one square sail on a mast stepped about amidships. Curiously, there were two British survivals of single-masted square-riggers into the twentieth century. These were the Humber keel – one was still sailing as late as 1949 – and small boats in the oyster trade on the River Roach and adjoining creeks of Essex until the First World War, the latter being the home waters of our original ketches. It is quite probable that 'Ferdes cache' of 1481 had just such a rig. Rather than dreaming up her possible appearance it is better to portray an authentic survival hence Fig 33 shows a typical Humber keel but it does not take much imagination to consider the small 'pink' in Fig 14 as a single-masted decked vessel, perhaps a ketch.

If, in addition to her sail plan, proof is needed of the keel's antiquity we can note that her shrouds were set up by lanyards rove through melon seed-shaped deadeyes, the type in common use on Elizabethan vessels. Further, each sail was secured to its yard in the old manner by robands that passed entirely around the yard. The keel's running rigging, however, was kept up to date and her handling by a crew of two was aided by the extensive use of wire rope and hand winches.

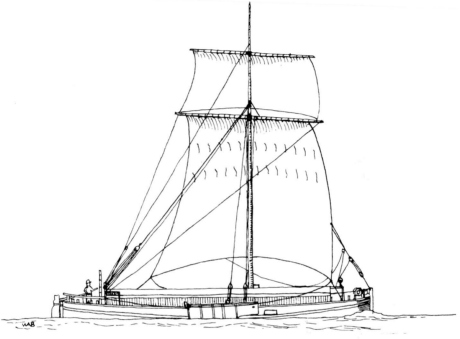

33. *Humber keel – after Carr*, Sailing Barges

As long as the ketch's principal employment was on creeks, rivers, and estuaries where the tide played an important role in her goings and comings, a single-masted square rig would have been adequate. It would also have been adequate for occasional coastwise passages. But we need not assume that all cargo carriers on the rivers and estuaries of eastern England in the late 1400s had single-masted square rigs, for the fore-and-aft spritsail was known by that time.

Until about 1960 it had been assumed that the fore-and-aft spritsail was invented by the Dutch but studies of Greek carvings disclosed the use of this sail in the eastern Mediterranean region as early as the second century BC.[17] The question now is whether the lack of artists' interest in familiar small craft can be blamed for the absence of pictorial evidence for the continued use of this sail. Considering that the preponderance of art in the Middle Ages was of a religious nature this probably is the reason; when vessels were shown, the artists preferred the larger and more important types.

Be that as it may, an early portrayal of the fore-and-aft spritsail in northern Europe appears in a religious work, *Les tres belles heures de Notre Dame*, considered to be the work of Hubrecht van Eyck in 1416–17 for Jean de France, duc de Berry. The craft carrying this sail is a small open, single-masted double-ender, perhaps about twenty feet long. She is shown from the port quarter with the wind on her starboard quarter and the spritsail well out to port.[18]

About fifty years later we can find a portrayal of a small vessel that meets some of our requirements for a ketch as she apparently is a flush-decked double-ender. As sketched in Fig 34 from a Flemish *Gestes de César* of the late fifteenth century, her crew is setting her sprit mainsail. The men appear a little too large in scale but the size of the small boat alongside corrects this to a certain extent. This vessel probably carried a staysail forward and the line coming aft from the forestay could be its sheet.[19] In view of the apparent widespread use of the single-masted fore-and-aft rig on Continental waters in the late 1400s, I believe that it was also employed on the waters of eastern England where the rivers and estuaries were similar to those of the Low Countries and handy cargo vessels were required. Therefore it is equally probable that 'Ferdes cache' was so rigged and may have looked something like Fig 34. This rig, of course, is the same as that carried by the pinnace *Virginia*, Fig 13.

34. *Flush deck vessel with spritsail, fifteenth century – after RMN,* The Mariner's Mirror, 6

THE COLONIAL KETCH

The earliest pictorial representation definitely labelled 'A Ketch' is a drawing in the log of Dr Thomas Browne, dated 1661–62, shown in Fig 35. The following description of her is from *The Mariner's Mirror*, 3 (1913), 55:

> She is shown with a good deal of rake to her stem. Her stern is not clearly outlined, but seems to be round. There are two hances in her rail abaft the mainmast, as though she had a quarter deck and poop. The mainmast is stepped more than a third of her length on deck from the stem, but is well forward of amidships. She has a running bowsprit on the starboard side of her stem head, and at the end of it is a small staff. Well aft is a small mizzenmast, carrying a lateen. There is a main topmast in length rather more than half the distance from the maintop or crosstrees, which she has is not clear, to the deck. Her sails are a large square mainsail with eyelet holes in the foot, a square topsail much smaller in proportion to the mainsail than was then usual in ships, a fore staysail, the tack of which comes well abaft the stem, perhaps an error of observation, a low-footed jib with its tack about one-third in from the bowsprit end, and the mizzen before mentioned. Both jib and fore staysail are shown on the wrong side of the mainsail. Trust cannot be put in details but the ratlines of the main shrouds are put in with some care.

Since the 1920s a carved stone relief panel of what is essentially the same vessel bearing the caption:

NONSUCH
CAPTAIN ZACHARY GILLAM
SAILED FROM GRAVESEND FOR HUDSON BAY
3RD JUNE 1668

has been on view above the main entrance of the London headquarters of the group incorporated on 2 May 1670 as 'The Governor and Company of Adventurers of England Trading into Hudson's Bay'. This incorporation followed the successful voyage of the ketch *Nonsuch* into Hudson's Bay from which she returned with a cargo of furs in October 1669.

One of the problems of marine research has been the sequence of the addition of other masts and sails to the basic single-masted square-rigger to arrive at the basic three-masted ship rig but it is easy to trace the development to this ketch of 1661–62. The obvious first addition was a lateen mizzen to aid in steering. Pictorial evidence for such a rig is no problem, for it was widely employed and an example from 1545 is sketched in Fig 36. We do not know, however, whether all vessels so rigged were called ketches or on how small a craft such a rig was fitted.

THE MAYFLOWER

35. 'A Ketch' – after Dr Browne, 1661–62

In one or more steps three other sails were added – a staysail forward, a small topsail, and a spritsail under the bowsprit. We have already seen this rig in Fig 21, which can be dated about 1585, on a vessel that we classed as a pinnace. There is evidence that in 1631 it was the rig of a ketch. In August 1631 sailmaker William Cottwen received payment for a suit of ketch sails of this description furnished to John Winthrop, Jr, son of the governor of the Massachusetts Bay colony. This suit of sails consisted of a mainsail with two bonnets, a foresail (staysail) with a bonnet, a topsail, a mizzen (lateen), and a spritsail under the bowsprit. The main- and foresails were of heavy canvas while the other three were of light cloth which amounted to only 32 percent of the total cloth used.[20] These sails might have been for the bark *Blessing of the Bay* which would complicate our bark story. While usually considered the first vessel built in the colony another, in one reference also called a bark, had been constructed prior to 28 May 1629. In 1630, however, she was referred to as a pinnace and was likely the craft for which the ketch sails were provided.[21] To move from this 1631 ketch rig to Dr Browne's ketch of 1661–62 we need only substitute a jib for the spritsail under the bowsprit.

About thirty years after Dr Browne's sketch the artist Isaac Sailmaker included a naval ketch or royal yacht in his painting of HMS *Britannia*. This little vessel is sketched in Fig 37 and we can see immediately that her rig differs considerably from that of the bomb-

130

ketch in Fig 32 of about the same date. The sails on the latter's mainmast have the proportions of those of a ship of the period while Sailmaker showed the deep narrow main and small higher sails of older types.

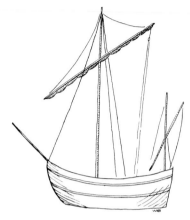

36. *Vessel in Portsmouth harbor, 1545 – after Basire in Bowen*, The Sea

In his book *The Ship-builder's Assistant* (London, 1711) William Sutherland, 'Shipwright and Mariner', included the sail plan and outboard profile of 'A Yacht, or Pleasure Boat' that has often been published as an example of a ketch. He also published mast and spar proportions for a ketch that, however, produce a different rig, one having the characteristics shown by Dr Browne and Sailmaker, the deep narrow mainsail and small topsail. The same features could be seen on a model of a bomb-ketch c1720 formerly in the Science Museum, London; its present location is not known.

A parallel development can be traced from the sprit mainsail and staysail rig of Fig 34. Again the first addition was a lateen mizzen; vessels with this rig are shown in a view of Calais dated 1545 and on a map of Rye of 1572. To this we need only add a square topsail – they were carried by English hoys in 1616 – and a jib to reach the fore-and-aft equivalent of Dr Browne's 'A Ketch'. He showed just such a rig in a sketch called 'A Galliot', Fig 38. Her mainsail is a slightly later development having a standing gaff that originally was called a half sprit but her hull is essentially the same double-ender as that of 'A Ketch'. The same rig is shown on a more elaborate square-sterned hull in another sketch titled 'A Yacht'.

Dassie, in his *L'Architecture Navale* of 1677, gives perhaps the earliest French definition of a ketch. The French had become aware of the English word and several variations were devised to approximate its pronunciation – *quesche*, *quaiche*, and *caiche* are samples. Whether they applied these variations to the English merchant type exclusively or to something of their own that was similar may never be known. What the English called a bomb-ketch was to the French a 'galiote aux bombes'. There was, however, more confusion than might appear from this. Dassie introduced a new type name, 'tronc', that appears in no other work. According to him, the 'tronc' and the 'quesche' were essentially the same except that the 'tronc' had a square rig (Figs 21 and 35) while that of the 'quesche' was fore-and-aft (Figs 20 and 38). The fact that the new name was applied to the square rig may be of significance in the sequence of development. Quillet and Aubin, as might be expected, again have essentially the same definition – a ketch was a single-decked vessel which had a gaff and a fore-and-aft rig like a yacht or a hoy, ie the same as Dr Browne's 'A Galliot', Fig 38.

37. Naval ketch or royal yacht, c1692 – after I Sailmaker

38. 'A Galliot' – after Dr Browne, 1661–62

Now the sails on the mainmast of Dr Browne's ketch – a deep narrow mainsail and a small topsail – do not look like anything that might have been adopted from a ship where the hoist of the topsail was close to the depth of the course. They are, however, what might be expected if the fore-and-aft mainsail of his galliot, Fig 38, was replaced by a square mainsail in preparation for an ocean voyage or for some other reason as we already have noted in connection with the bojorts in Chapter 4. The 1631 sailmaker's bill might apply equally well to this fore-and-aft rig as there is no indication in it whether the mainsail was square or a spritsail.

Turning finally to the rig of colonial North American ketches we can eliminate first the often suggested lateen for the reasons given in the first chapter. For years photographs of the model from which Fig 39 was sketched were used whenever anyone wanted a representation of a seventeenth-century New England fishing ketch. I think that this can be eliminated too, for the crews of the sixty Salem fishing ketches of 1697 mentioned earlier in this chapter averaged five or six and they went out to fish, not to handle sail.

Knowing that New England ketches made voyages to Newfoundland, the Azores, Madeira, and the West Indies as well as long coastal passages and having accepted John Foster's 1677 map as evidence for a two-masted square rig we must accept his portrait of the large

133

39. American fishing ketch – after Smithsonian Catalog, 1923

square-rigged ketch shown in Fig 40 as proof of such a rig in New England waters. Such a rig might well have been carried by the 80-ton *Dove* that in 1688 sailed from Boston to Maryland with a crew of ten. On the other hand the same rig would have been absurd on the ketch *Prosperous* that cleared from Boston for Jamaica in 1687; she measured only 6 tons and had a crew of four. This ketch was the smallest of at least 100 ketches that sailed on trading voyages from Boston in 1687–88. Based on the proportions of the 1678 ketch built by William Carr her length overall could have been 26ft, her breadth 7ft 8in, and her depth 3ft 9in but such a small vessel might actually have been a bit shorter and deeper. I suggest that small ketches like the *Prosperous* had the same single-masted fore-and-aft rig that was used on the *Pilgrim Shallop II* and the pinnace *Virginia*. Possibly the small vessel shown off the mouth of the Piscataqua River on John Foster's 1677 map, Fig 41, was intended to represent such a ketch.

A crew of four was the smallest given for any of the 100 ketches that sailed from Boston but in this listing that number handled ketches that ranged in size from the 6-ton *Prosperous* up to 30-tonners. Some of the latter, however, had crews of as many as eight men which might indicate a different rig. In other words, a fore-and-aft rigged 30-ton ketch may have had a crew of four while a square-rigged ketch of the same size might have required a crew of eight. A 30-ton ketch would have been slightly larger than that built by William Carr.

40. *Large ketch – after Foster*

Governor Winthrop's first reference to a ketch tends to support a fore-and-aft rig. On 17 May 1640:[22]

Joseph Grafton set sail from Salem, the 2d day in the morning, in a ketch of about forty tons (three men and a boy in her), and arrived at Pemaquid (the wind easterly) upon the third day in the morning, and there took in some twenty cows, oxen, etc, with hay and water for them and came to an anchor in the bay the 6th day about three after noon.

41. *Small ketch – after Foster*

This must have been an unusual performance to have been recorded in this fashion. From other references to the weather and storms Winthrop seems to have been fairly precise in giving wind directions.

With the wind easterly the ketch would have had to sail from Cape Ann to Pemaquid on a fairly close reach. A square-rigger just might have done it without further tacking once clear of the cape; a fore-and-aft rigged vessel could have done it with ease. And the crew of four – one a boy – supports the conclusion that Grafton's ketch was fore-and-aft rigged.

The shortest possible route from Salem to Pemaquid in the present State of Maine is 105 miles. With the wind easterly some beating would have been necessary to clear Cape Ann hence several miles must be added to this figure. For a morning to morning passage from Salem to Pemaquid Grafton's ketch would have had to average a bit better than 4½kts. This would be a good performance for a modern cruising yacht and it indicates that the ketch must have had a relatively fine form.

In 1676–77 we can find another instance of a ketch handled by a small crew. In connection with concerted efforts by the natives to obtain small vessels with which to destroy the colonists' fishing fleet, a 30-ton ketch was captured by them off Richmond Island near Cape Elizabeth on the coast of Maine. Her crew was held for ransom. This capture occurred in October 1676, too late for operations against the fishing fleet, so the ketch was sailed to the Sheepscot River and laid up for the winter.

The following spring, with one of the colonists, John Abbott, as sailing master and ten natives to sail and fight her, the ketch put to sea. Caught in a gale she was driven into the harbor of Cape Newagen where eight of the natives departed. Putting to sea again with a crew of three another gale drove the ketch into Damariscove. Abbott finally sailed her single-handed from there to the Isles of Shoals, a distance of about 65 miles. In extreme circumstances many things are possible but such single-handed sailing indicates a fore-and-aft rather than a square rig.[23]

Winthrop's *History* and other sources affirm the employment of ketches as carriers along the New England coast but I believe that it was the easily handled, efficient fore-and-aft rig of the smaller ketches in combination with their easily driven double-ended forms that led to their wide use for offshore fishing. The more or less open shallops were the inshore fishing boats. The important fishing grounds were 'down east' off the coast of Maine and any modern yachtsman knows how easy it is to sail 'down east' from Boston or Salem. Most of the time it is a pleasant down-wind sail but the problem was and is to return against the prevailing south-westerly winds in summer and the northwesterlies in winter. The advantages of a fore-and-aft rig over a square rig are readily apparent.

As a further clincher to the argument in favor of a widespread use of a fore-and-aft rig on colonial New England ketches H I Chapelle has noted, based on Custom House records of New England fishing vessels, that between 1710 and 1720 ketches were rather suddenly replaced by schooners.[24] American tradition places the invention of the schooner in the year 1713 although examples of vessels having the two-masted fore-and-aft rig (fore and mainmasts with a triangular headsail) that was supposed to differentiate schooners from other vessels can be found over fifty years earlier.

It is unreasonable to assume that the majority of the fishing ketches were scrapped and new schooners built during the above mentioned decade or even that a wholesale re-rigging occurred. It is more likely that a newly fashionable type name was adopted for as many somewhat similar vessels as possible and one or two features may have been adopted at the same time. This happened during the clipper ship craze in the middle 1800s when all but the very slowest of cargo ships were advertised as being at least medium clippers. It is interesting to recall that the type name schooner, originally scooner, which now applies to a rig, was based on a quality of form, the way the first of the type 'scooned' or skimmed over the water at launching. The traditional story of the invention of the schooner now seems apocryphal and the origin of the verb 'to scoon' has never been traced. Further, it was not until 1716 that schooners were mentioned in Boston and Gloucester records; Boston's was listed under entries on 4 May: 'James Manson ye Skooner Mayflower from North Carolina.'

It is probable that the assumed invention of the schooner at Gloucester in 1713 consisted of fitting the long known two-masted fore-and-aft Dutch rig – the fore and main mast combination with a triangular headsail – on a typical ketch hull. While the larger New England fishing vessels and the coastal traders quickly adopted this rig with the mainsail larger than the fore and were henceforth called schooners it is worth noting that many of the smaller craft retained the main and mizzen pattern of the ketch, with or without triangular headsail, until the internal combustion engine replaced sail as motive power. It is quite probable that the schooner-rigged double-ended New England pinky was the final development of the colonial fishing ketch.

I suggest that the small barks and ketches built by the North American colonists during the first two-thirds of the seventeenth century were much alike in form and construction. Both were single-

XIX. *On board the* Adventure – *detail of windlass.* (Author)

decked vessels, basically double-enders. By late in the century the majority of the barks had adopted the square stern as they and other types replaced pinnaces but ketches remained double-enders. In general ketches were smaller than barks but there was some overlap in the size range. Given a bark and a ketch of the same burden it is probable that the latter had the finer underbody.

While I believe that barks always were square-rigged, ketches – like pinnaces – may have had a variety of rigs. To the seventeenth-century North American colonists the term ketch probably defined a hull rather than a rig but certain rigs were likely more or less associated with the type within three size ranges. There is enough scattered evidence to prove, in the latter part of the seventeenth century at least, that large ketches carrying a square-rigged mainmast and a smaller fore-and-aft-rigged mizzen, occasionally with a square topsail, could be seen in North American waters. At the other end of the scale I believe that the smallest ketches carried only the single-masted sprit mainsail and fore staysail rig. Ketches in the middle of the size range had a two-masted fore-and-aft rig arranged with main and mizzen masts. Fig 42 might represent such a ketch.

On Monday, 27 April 1970, a sleek motor yacht from Annapolis, Maryland, hailed an unusual vessel under sail in the harbor of Charleston, South Carolina:

'What are you?' — 'A seventeenth-century ketch.'

'Where are you going?' — 'We're lost.'

'You've been lost a long time!' came the final retort.

The ketch was the *Adventure* that I designed and had built for the South Carolina Tricentennial Commission as part of the state's celebration of the founding of its first settlement on the west bank of the Ashley River early in April 1670. During the next decade the colonists moved across the river to the peninsula between the Ashley and Cooper Rivers that is the present Charleston; it became the seat of the colony's government in the spring of 1680. The site of the original settlement reverted to nature and remained relatively untouched for years; it is now part of a park known as Charles Towne Landing. In Old Town Creek, just below a reconstruction of the earthworks that were erected by the colonists for protection against the Spanish, the *Adventure* is normally moored to a small wharf as were her ancestors three centuries ago. Instead of sailing to Barbados with cargoes of logs, shingles, staves, tobacco, tar, beef, and pork and returning with sugar and molasses she is a permanent exhibit of life at sea in the late seventeenth century.

THE MAYFLOWER

The only stipulation by the Tricentennial Commission concerning the design of the *Adventure* was that she be large enough to permit visitors to walk through her hold. This requirement set her depth at 8ft. The 1666 and 1678 contracts for Massachusetts-built ketches quoted earlier provided suitable proportions and some details. As finally worked out this new seventeenth-century ketch has a keel length of 37ft and a maximum breadth inside the planking of 14ft 4in; her overall hull length is 53ft. By the tonnage rule of her day she measures 43 tons. She is named the *Adventure* after a late seventeenth-century ketch of the same size known to have traded along the Atlantic coast of North America from Newfoundland on the north as far as Barbados to the south; she would be quite capable of sailing to the Azores and Madeira as did other ketches of the period.

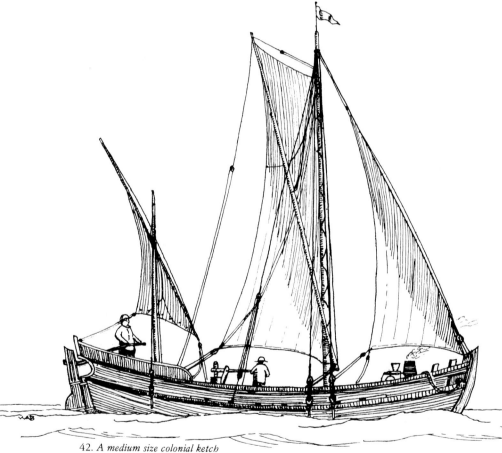

42. *A medium size colonial ketch*

THE COLONIAL KETCH

In developing the *Adventure*'s hull form I took a cue from the early eighteenth-century *Lexicon Technicum* by John Harris in which he stated that a ketch was 'a smaller vessel, but of the same form with a Hoy'. Ake Classon Ralamb's *Skeps Byggerij* of 1691, which reported on shipbuilding practices in England and the Netherlands included the lines of an English hoy of the late 1680s. These lines were the basis for those of the *Adventure* but the latter are a bit finer. Photographs of the bomb-ketch model formerly in London's Science Museum supplied some useful details.

The *Adventure*'s arrangement is simple. On deck forward is a log windlass and immediately abaft it is a small hatch which serves for access to the 'forecastle' below as well as for passing down the anchor cable. Just abaft the mainmast is the large cargo hatch and between it and the quarter deck is a log pump. The quarter deck is raised one foot above the main deck to give a little more space in the cabin below.

The 'forecastle' at the forward end of the cargo hold contains four built-in berths, a brick hearth for cooking, and space for stores. Smoke from the cooking fire is supposed to find its way out through a portable wooden chimney in the deck over. The cabin aft, reached through a hatch in the raised quarter deck, has four more built-in berths. Normally a bulkhead would separate the cabin and cargo hold but this was omitted to give visitors a better view.

The *Adventure*'s keel was laid early in June 1969 by master builder James B Richardson in the building shed of his yard at Lloyds, Dorchester County, Maryland, just west of Cambridge. Construction proceeded steadily during the following summer, autumn, and winter. With only inches to spare the new ketch was moved out of the shed on 9 March 1970 and during the next few days positioned on Richardson's marine railway ready for launching. 'Time and tide wait for no man' but Chesapeake Bay tides are unpredictable and men waited until the afternoon of 20 March to ease the *Adventure* into the waters of Le Comte's Creek. In keeping with the tradition established by the *Mayflower II* and the *Pilgrim Shallop II* this launching also took place during a heavy downpour. Because of the restricted depth of water in the creek no ballast could be put in the ketch but she floated upright and gave me no additional gray hairs.

The new ketch has double sawn-futtock framing with built-up deadwood at the ends instead of the seventeenth-century natural grown Y-timbers. Among the obvious seventeenth-century features, however, are the details of the deck framing and the hanging knees secured to the sides of the beams. To aid in maintenance and preservation the usual ceiling was omitted. The *Adventure*'s framing and planking are of oak, deck beams of pine, knees of hackmatack (larch), decking of fir, and bulwarks, bulkheads and berths of cypress.

The *Adventure* was towed from Le Comte's Creek to Cambridge's Long Wharf where nearly 19 tons of iron and stone ballast were put in her hold. On 24 March with her spars lashed on deck she departed for Charleston, South Carolina, in tow of a US Navy tug of half again her length. By 4 April, the beginning of the tricentennial celebration, she was moored at Charles Towne Landing and partially rigged. Nearly all of April was needed to complete the rigging and bend the sails.

The lengths and diameters of the *Adventure*'s masts and spars are based on the proportions set down by Sutherland, which were over forty years old when he published them in 1711, except that the length of the mizzen mast was reduced as indicated by the spar dimensions of ketch-rigged yachts of the 1670s.[25] For maintenance reasons all of her rigging is of synthetic materials. As shown by Fig 43 the *Adventure* carries the same five sails as Dr Browne's ketch of 1661–62. Because of her size there was no need to consider a possible fore-and-aft rig.

As noted earlier the big day came on 27 April 1970 when with a crew of a dozen volunteers, experienced yachtsmen and others, the *Adventure* went out for sailing trials in Charleston's outer harbor. She was towed from Charles Towne Landing down through the Ashley River bridges while the confusing 'strings' were sorted out by a crew accustomed to stainless wire rigging and chrome-plated winches. When clear of the bridges the jib and mizzen were soon set and the tug cast off: the *Adventure* was on her own for the first time. The mainsail was then hoisted and she sailed easily down the Ashley against the tide with a 10–12kt breeze on her starboard quarter.

Any vessel can move with the wind but what would the *Adventure* do to windward? In lower Charleston Harbor she was put close-hauled on the starboard tack and moved well at about five points off the wind. But would she tack? The helm was put down and the jib sheet let go. She came slowly into the wind; the mainsail came aback and the jib was sheeted to port to help her around. As the *Adventure* swung through the eye of the wind the jib was sheeted home on the port tack, the main yard was swung by the braces, the port tack boarded, and the starboard sheet hauled in and belayed. The mizzen was shifted to the lee side of the mast and she was off again. All on board breathed a sigh of relief but none deeper than mine for I was in command and on the spot; she could be tacked. After a few more maneuvers the sails were lowered and the *Adventure* was towed to a Shem Creek shipyard on the north side of the harbor to be hauled out for bottom inspection.

On Thursday, 30 April, the *Adventure* sailed again in a 15–20kt easterly and performed even better. The topsail, set flying from the deck, proved efficient on all points of sailing. With a draft of a bit under 6ft, relatively light for a vessel of her size, she made some leeway but because of the tidal currents the amount was difficult to judge. On this day with the main bowline set up and the lee rigging slack she headed four points (45°) off the wind and probably made good five points at a speed of five to six knots. Her weather helm at

43. *The* Adventure

the time was only 4in at the end of the 7ft tiller. With her working crew down to seven, a more normal size, the *Adventure* was tacked several times in a little over a minute each time. In the late afternoon she headed back up the Ashley River. Her sails were furled one by one, the tug came alongside, and she was towed back to Charles Towne Landing. Seventeenth-century writers noted the handiness of ketches; the *Adventure* has proved them correct.

Summary

Now that arguments concerning seventeenth-century shallops, pinnaces, barks, and ketches have been presented (not all by any means, but enough for these studies), a few words in summary might be useful. Ships are well enough known and defined that they need not be included. I hope that in the preceding pages it has been apparent that no one- or two-line definition can describe any particular vessel type, even a ship, over a considerable number of years. Because of the inevitable variations from builder to builder, neither can a brief definition apply to all vessels known by a given type name at any definite date. Even with our present day loose classification of sailing vessels by rig only simple definitions cannot cover all possible variations. In the following paragraphs I have attempted to summarize my understanding of the above four types as they existed during the first seventy-five years of the English colonies in New England.

Shallop. A heavily-constructed, double-ended work boat, open or partially decked, propelled by both oars and sails and employed for in-shore fishing and limited coastwise trading. Shallops had either (a) a single-masted fore-and-aft rig comprised of a sprit mainsail and a stay-sail or (b) a two-masted square rig having a deep narrow mainsail on a mast stepped nearly amidships and a small foresail on a mast stepped well forward.

Pinnace. A lightly-built, single-decked, square-sterned vessel generally having superstructures forward and aft, ie forecastle and poop. Pinnaces ranged in size from 12 to 200 tons and were suitable for light naval duties, as tenders to large exploring or trading ships, or for independent voyages. Although primarily sailing vessels, pinnaces often were equipped with sweeps for use in calm weather or for moving around in harbors. Rigs of pinnaces ranged from the simple sprit main- and staysail combination to the full ship rig of the period. Vessels classed as pinnaces were employed by the North American colonists for fishing and coastwise trading and, to a limited extent, for carrying cargo and passengers to and from England.

Bark. A single-decked, often round-sterned vessel without super-structures. Barks ranged in size from 12 to 100 tons and were employed for coastwise trading and some fishing. In general barks had a two-masted square rig similar to that described under (b) for shallops. Small barks had only these sails; medium-sized barks probably carried small topsails as well, while the largest barks had topsails and a small lateen mizzen.

Ketch. A strongly-built, beamy, flush-decked, round-sterned vessel. Ketches ranged in size from 6 to 80 tons but the average was close to 30 tons. They formed the bulk of the colonists' off-shore fishing fleet in the second half of the seventeenth century; many were employed in trading to Newfoundland, the Azores, the Madeiras, and the West Indies. The rig varied with size and service. For small ketches it may have been the same as that described under (a) for the shallop or perhaps only a single deep, narrow, square sail on a mast stepped nearly amidships. Medium size ketches had a fore-and-aft rig consisting of one or two triangular headsails, a sprit main, and a lateen or sprit mizzen. Larger ketches had a square sail under the bowsprit (that was superseded by a jib), a staysail, a small square topsail, and a lateen mizzen. They carried sprit mainsails for coastal work and deep, narrow, square sails for off-shore work.

PLANS FOR MODEL BUILDERS

Plans suitable for model builders are available for the following vessels mentioned in this volume:

1. *Mayflower II* – ship c1600 – four $1/8$in scale plans, rigging specifications, and various details.

2. Colonial Bark c1640 – three $1/4$in scale plans and rigging specifications.

Both are available from Plimoth Plantation, Inc, Box 1620, Plymouth, Mass, USA, 02360, and selected dealers in ship model supplies.

3. *Concord* – Bartholomew Gosnold's ship-rigged bark of 1602 – four plans and rigging specifications.

4. Shallop in halves, carried on the *Concord* – one plan.

These two sets may be purchased from the Old Dartmouth Historical Society, 18 Johnny Cake Hill, New Bedford, Mass, USA, 02740.

Appendices

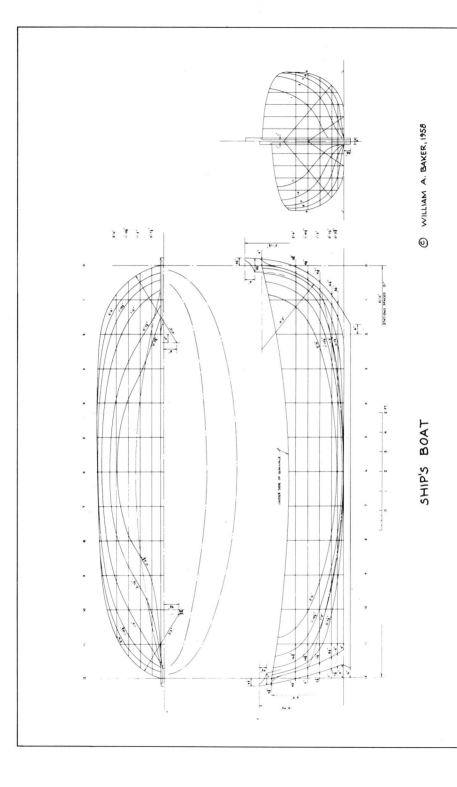

© WILLIAM A. BAKER, 1958

SHIP'S BOAT

SHIP'S BOAT

© WILLIAM A. BAKER, 1958

APPENDIX B

RIGGING

The order of listing the various items roughly follows the procedure of rigging — first, tackle pendants, then shrouds, stays, rigging pertaining to the yards, and finally rigging pertaining to sails.

1. GAMMONING — 4½in circ 1½in diam common lay — about 8 turns. Stop cleats fitted on bowsprit to keep from slipping.
2. MAIN TACKLE — port and starboard.
   Pendant — 6in circ 2in diam shroud lay. Upper end — served eye splice over masthead.
   Lower end — single block for runner seized in.
   Runner — 4½in circ 1½in diam common lay. Lower end — hooked to eyebolt on main channel. Reeve through pendant block and seize in fiddle block at upper end.
   Falls — 3in circ 1in diam common lay. Lower block of purchase — rope strapped single with becket and hook to eyebolt on main channel. Belayed to timber head or pin rail under shrouds.
3. FORE TACKLE — port and starboard.
   Pendant — 4½in circ 1½in diam shroud lay. Upper end — served eye splice over masthead.
   Lower end — single block for runner seized in.
   Runner — 3½in circ 1⅛in diam common lay. Lower end — hooked to eyebolt on fore channel. Reeve through pendant block and seize in fiddle block at upper end.
   Falls — 2½in circ 13/16in diam common lay. Lower block of purchase — rope strapped single with becket and hook to eyebolt on fore channel. Belayed to timber head or pin rail under shrouds.
4. MAIN SHROUDS — port and starboard, 7 per side — 6in circ 2in diam shroud lay. Upper end — served seized loop for three pair; served eye splice or cut splice for odd shroud. Lower end — 3 hole deadeye.
   Laniards — 3½in circ 1⅛in diam common lay.
   Ratlines — 1½in circ ½in diam common lay. Fitted to all shrouds — clove hitched to each shroud — ends seized.
   On channels — 3 hole deadeyes with 1⅜in diam iron straps 1⅜in diam long link chain with 1⅝in diam bolt to hull.
5. FORE SHROUDS — port and starboard, 5 per side — 4½in circ 1½in diam shroud lay. Upper end — served seized loops for two pair; served eye splice or cut splice for odd shroud. Lower end — 3 hole deadeye.
   Laniards — 2¾in circ ⅞in diam common lay.
   Ratlines — 1½in circ ½in diam common lay. Clove hitched to each shroud — ends seized.
   On channels — 3 hole deadeyes with 1⅛in diam iron straps, 1⅛in diam long link chain with 1⅜in diam bolt to hull.
6. MIZZEN SHROUDS — port and starboard, 3 per side — 2¾in circ ⅞in diam shroud lay. Upper end — served seized loop for one pair; served eye splice or cut splice for odd shroud. Lower end — 3 hole deadeye.

Laniards — 1½in circ ½in diam common lay.

Ratlines — 1½in circ ½in diam common lay. Clove hitched to each shroud — ends seized.

On channels — 3 hole deadeyes with ¾in diam iron straps, ¾in diam long link chain with 1in diam bolt to hull.

7. MAIN STAY — 10in circ 3¼in diam cabled. Upper end — eye and mouse to form loop over masthead — loop served. Lower end — 5 hole deadeye.

Collar — 9in circ 3in diam cabled. 5 hole deadeye seized in. Collar passed around foremast and through hole in upper stem knee. Ends have seized eyes lashed together.

Laniard — 4in circ 15/16in diam common lay.

8. FORE STAY — 9in circ 3in dia cabled. Upper end — eye and mouse to form loop over masthead — loop served. Lower end — 5 hole deadeye.

Collar — 8in circ 2⅝in diam cabled. Secured around bowsprit against stop cleat. 5 hole deadeye seized in.

Laniard — 3½in circ 1⅛in diam common lay.

9. MIZZEN STAY — 5in circ 1⅝in diam cabled. Upper end — eye and mouse to form loop over masthead — loop served. Lower end — 3 hole deadeye.

Collar — 4½in circ 1½in diam cabled. Secured around mainmast against stop cleat. 3 hole deadeye seized in.

Laniard — 2½in circ 13/16in diam common lay.

10. TOP ROPE — MAIN TOPMAST — 4in circ $1\frac{5}{16}$in diam common lay. Standing part secured to eyebolt under mainmast cap, port side. Reeve through sheave in heel of topmast to single block under mainmast cap, starboard side, then through hole in top to main knight and capstan. Coil in top when not in use.

11. TOP ROPE — FORE TOPMAST — 3½in circ 1⅛in diam common lay. Same as for main topmast to opposite hand.

12. MAIN TOPMAST TACKLE — port and starboard.

Pendant — 3½in circ 1⅛in diam common lay. Upper end — served eye splice over masthead. Lower end — single block for falls seized in.

Falls — 3in circ 1in diam common lay. One end hooked at forward puttock plate — other end belayed around after deadeye on rim of main top.

13. FORE TOPMAST TACKLE — port and starboard.

Pendant — 3in circ 1in diam common lay. Upper end — served eye splice over masthead. Lower end — single block for falls seized in.

Falls — 2½in circ 13/16in diam common lay. One end hooked at forward puttock plate — other end belayed around after deadeye on rim of fore top.

14. MAIN TOPMAST SHROUDS — port and starboard, 3 per side — 3½in circ 1⅛in diam shroud lay. Upper end — served seized loop for one pair; served eye splice or cut splice for odd shroud. Lower end — 3 hole deadeye.

Laniards — 2in circ ⅝in diam common lay.

Ratlines — 1⅛in circ ⅜in diam common lay. Clove hitched to each shroud — ends seized.

On rim of top — 3 hole deadeyes with ¾in diam iron straps hooked to 15in × 2½in × ¾in iron puttock plates passing through rim.

Futtock shrouds — 3½in circ 1⅛in diam shroud lay. Upper end — eye with thimble and hook to puttock plate. Lower end — secured to futtock pole and seized to main shrouds.

15. FORE TOPMAST SHROUDS — port and starboard, 3 per side — 3in circ 1in diam shroud lay. Upper end — served seized loop for one pair; served eye splice or cut splice for odd shroud. Lower end — 3 hole deadeyes.
Laniards — 1½in circ ½in diam common lay.
Ratlines — 1⅛in circ ⅜in diam common lay. Clove hitched to each shroud — ends seized.
On rim of top — 3 hole deadeyes with ½in diam iron straps hooked to 12in × 1⅞in × ½in iron puttock plates passing through rim.
Futtock shrouds — 3in circ 1in diam shroud lay. Upper end — eye with thimble and hook to puttock plate. Lower end — secured to futtock pole and seized to fore shrouds.

16. MAIN TOPMAST STAY — 5in circ 1⅝in diam cabled. Upper end — eye and mouse to form loop over masthead — loop served. Lower end — 3 hole deadeye.
Collar — 4in circ 1 5/16in diam common lay. Seized in 3 hole deadeye. Secure to fore masthead.
Laniard — 3¼in circ 1 1/16in diam common lay.

17. FORE TOPMAST STAY — 4in circ 1 5/16in diam cabled. Upper end — eye and mouse to form loop over masthead — loop served.
Lower end — single block for pendant.
Pendant — 3in circ 1in diam common lay. Outboard end — served eye around bowsprit with stop cleat. Inboard end — single block for runner.
Runner — 2¼in circ ¾in diam common lay. Outboard end — served eye around bowsprit with stop cleat about 3ft inboard of pendant. Reeve through pendant block to lead block on bowsprit. Belayed to cleat on bowsprit port side near gammoning.

18. MAIN TOPMAST BACKSTAYS — port and starboard, 1 per side.
Pendant — 2½in circ 13/16in diam common lay. Upper end — served eye splice or cut splice over masthead. Lower end — single block for falls.
Falls — 2in circ ⅝in diam common lay. One end secured to eyebolt on halfdeck rail stanchion — reeve through pendant block. Belayed to timber head on halfdeck.

19. FORE TOPMAST BACKSTAYS — port and starboard, 1 per side.
Pendant — 2in circ ⅝in diam common lay. Upper end — served eye splice or cut splice over masthead. Lower end — single block for falls.
Falls — 1½in circ ½in diam common lay. One end secured to eyebolt on forecastle deck rail stanchion — reeve through pendant block. Belayed to timber head on forecastle deck.

20. MAIN YARD
Parrel — 3¾in circ 1¼in diam common lay. Fit 9 ribs and 24 trucks.
Ties — 5in circ 1⅝in diam shroud lay. Reeve through hounds and hole in ramhead block. Both ends hitched and seized to yard. Both parts seized together just above ramhead. Yard to have lashed-on mat to prevent galling of mast.

Halyard — 3in circ 1in diam common lay. Fixed end secured to eyebolt on port side of main knight — 6 parts to ramhead block. Belayed around head of knight.

Jeer — 4½in circ 1½in diam common lay. Standing part secured to masthead above shrouds — port side — passes inside main stay loop and outside of trestle trees through single block strapped to yard to single block under starboard trestle trees (secured by long pendant fastened above shrouds). Belayed on starboard main rail under shrouds.

Truss (downhaul) — 4½in circ 1½in diam common lay. Timber hitched to middle of yard. Led to capstan when needed through snatch block secured to deck ringbolt. Belayed to starboard main rail under shrouds.

Braces — port and starboard — Pendant — 4in circ 1 5/16in diam common lay — about 15ft long. Served eye splice over yard arm — single block for falls spliced or seized in other end. Falls — 2½in circ 13/16in diam common lay. Standing part secured to eyebolt on poop rail stanchion — hauling part returns from pendant through lead block on rail. Belayed to cleat on poop rail stanchion.

Lifts — port and starboard — 3in circ 1in diam common lay. Standing part secured to loop of mainstay — reeve through single block secured to strap of topsail sheet blocks to single block secured below trestle trees. Belayed to halfdeck rail under shrouds.

21. FORE YARD

Parrel — 3in circ 1in diam common lay. Fit 9 ribs and 24 trucks.

Ties — 4in circ 1 5/16in diam shroud lay. Reeve through hounds and hole in ramhead block — both ends hitched and seized to yard. Both parts seized together just above ramhead. Yard to have lashed-on mat to prevent galling of mast.

Halyard — 2½in circ 13/16in diam common lay. Fixed end secured to eyebolt on starboard side of fore knight — 6 parts to ramhead block. Belayed around head of knight.

Jeer — 3½in circ 1⅛in diam common lay. Standing part secured to masthead above shrouds — starboard side — passes inside fore stay loop outside of trestle trees through single block strapped to yard to single block under port trestle trees (secured by long pendant fastened above shrouds). Belayed to forecastle rail under shrouds — port side.

Truss (downhaul) — 3½in circ 1⅛in diam common lay. Timber hitched to middle of yard. Led to capstan when needed through snatch blocks secured to deck ringbolts. Belayed to forecastle rail under shrouds — port side.

Braces — port and starboard. Pendant — 3in circ 1in diam common lay — about 12ft long. Served eye splice over yard arm — single block for falls spliced or seized in other end. Falls — 2¼in circ ¾in diam common lay. Standing part secured to main stay about 21ft up from foremast — reeve through pendant block to lead block, secured to main stay about 3ft below standing part. Belayed on after forecastle rail. Lead blocks on stay spliced or seized into short span clove hitched to stay — 3in circ 1in diam common lay.

Lifts — port and starboard — 2½in circ 13/16in diam common lay. Standing part secured to loop of fore stay — reeve through single block secured to strap of topsail sheet block — to single block secured below trestle tree. Belayed to forecastle rail under shrouds.

22. MAIN TOPSAIL YARD

Parrel — 2¼in circ ¾in diam common lay. Fit 7 ribs and 12 trucks.

Tie — 5in circ 1⅝in diam shroud lay. One end hitched and seized to yard — reeve through hounds of topmast with single block for runner spliced or seized in other end.

Runner — 3½in circ 1⅛in diam common lay. Standing part hitched and seized to ringbolt near deck on port stanchion about 4ft forward of poop bulkhead — reeve through tie block with single block for halyard spliced or seized in other end.

Halyard — 2¾in circ ⅞in diam common lay. Standing part hooked to eyebolt near deck on starboard rail stanchion about 4ft forward of poop bulkhead — reeve through runner block. Belayed to cleat on halfdeck rail stanchion starboard side.

Braces — port and starboard. Pendant — 2½in circ 13/16in diam common lay — about 18ft long. Served eye splice over yard arm — single block for falls spliced or seized in other end. Falls — 2in circ ⅝in diam common lay. Standing part of falls hitched to mizzen masthead — reeve through pendant block to block secured to forward mizzen shroud about 6ft below trestle trees — then to block secured to after main shroud about 13ft above rail. Belayed to halfdeck rail under shrouds.

Lifts — port and starboard — 1½in circ ½in diam common lay. Standing part hitched to topmast head — reeve through single block at yard arm — to single block at topmast trestle tree. Belayed to cleat in main top.

23. FORE TOPSAIL YARD

Parrel — 2in circ ⅝in diam common lay. Fit 7 ribs and 12 trucks.

Tie — 4in circ 1 5/16in diam shroud lay. One end hitched and seized to yard — reeve through hounds of topmast with single block for runner spliced or seized in other end.

Runner — 2¾in circ ⅞in diam common lay. Standing part hitched and seized to ringbolt on starboard main rail stanchion abaft forecastle — reeve through tie block with single block for halyard spliced or seized in other end.

Halyard — 2in circ ⅝in diam common lay. Standing part hooked to eyebolt on port main rail stanchion abaft forecastle — reeve through runner block. Belayed to port rail.

Braces — port and starboard. Pendant — 2in circ ⅝in diam common lay — about 15ft long. Served eye splice over yard arm — single block for falls spliced or seized in other end. Falls — 1½in circ ½in diam common lay. Standing part hitched to main topmast stay about 22ft up from fore masthead — reeve through pendant block to lead block about 2½ft below standing part — to lead block on main stay about 1½ft below fore-brace lead block. Belayed on after forecastle rail. Lead blocks on stays spliced or seized into short spans clove hitched to stays — 2in circ ⅝in diam common lay.

Lifts — port and starboard — 1½in circ ½in diam common lay. Standing part hitched to topmast head — reeve through single block at yard arm — to single block at topmast trestle trees. Belayed to cleat in fore top.

24. SPRITSAIL YARD

Parrel — 3 in circ 1 in diam common lay. Fit 7 ribs and 12 trucks.

Halyard — 2½in circ 13/16in diam common lay. Standing part secured near outer end of bowsprit — reeve through single block secured to middle of yard to single block secured near standing part. Belayed to pin rail in beakhead — port side.

Lifts — port and starboard — 2¼in circ ¾in diam common lay. Standing part secured to 2½in circ 13/16in diam common lay pendant about 2ft long secured to end of bowsprit. Reeve through single block at yard arm to single block on bowsprit. Belayed to pin rail in beakhead.

Braces — port and starboard. Pendant — 2¼in circ ¾in diam common lay — about 4ft long. Served eye splice over yard arm — single block for falls spliced or seized in other end. Falls — 1½in circ ½in diam common lay. Standing part hitched to fore stay about 16ft below fore top. Reeve through pendant block to lead block on forestay about 1½ft below standing part to single block attached to beakhead rail. Belayed to pin rail in head.

Garnet — port and starboard — 2in circ ⅝in diam common lay. Standing part hitched to fore stay about 15in below brace block. Reeve through single block secured to yard midway between parrel and yard arm — to single block on stay about 1½ft below standing part to single block attached to beakhead rail. Belayed to pin rail in head.

25. MIZZEN YARD (LATEEN)

Parrel — 2¾in circ ⅞in diam common lay. Fit 7 ribs and 12 trucks.

Parrel downhaul — 3in circ 1in diam common lay. Belayed to cleat on mast.

Tie — 4in circ 1 5/16in diam shroud lay. One end hitched and seized to yard about 3ft below middle — reeve through hounds with single block for halyard seized in other end with becket.

Halyard — 2¾in circ ⅞in diam common lay. Standing part secured to becket on tie block — reeve from aft forward through knight — 3 parts. Belayed to head of knight.

Bowlines — port and starboard — 2½in circ 13/16in diam common lay. Standing part hitched to after main shroud about 10ft above rail — reeve through single block hooked to eye at lower end of yard to single block on shroud about 1½ft below standing part. Belayed on halfdeck rail.

Lift — Pendant — 3in circ 1in diam common lay — about 20ft long. Served eye over main topmast head — single block for runner spliced or seized in other end.

Lift — Runner — 2¼in circ ¾in diam common lay -- single block for falls seized in one end — reeve through pendant block to block at mizzen cross trees. Belayed to cleat on forward side of mast.

Lift — Falls — 2in circ ⅝in diam common lay. Single block for crane lines spliced or seized in each end — reeve through runner block.

Lift — Crane lines — 1½in circ ½in diam common lay. Ends hitched and seized to yard about 8ft apart — reeve through falls blocks and block hitched to yard midway between standing parts.

26. GARNET TACKLE

 Pendant — 6in circ 2in diam shroud lay. Hitched around main masthead above shrouds — lead outside trestle trees inside main stay loop to point over center of lower deck hatch — seized to main stay. Lower end — single block for runner.

 Runner — 4in circ 1 5/16in diam common lay. Reeve through pendant block — one end fitted with hook — fiddle block spliced or seized in other end.

 Falls — 2½in circ 13/16in diam common lay. Lower block of purchase — rope strapped single with becket and iron hook.

27. MAIN COURSE — head about 48ft — hoist including bonnet about 34ft. Bonnet about 11ft.

 Earings — 2in circ ⅝in diam common lay.

 Robands — braided line — passed through grommets under head rope of sail and tied around yard — spaced about 6in apart.

 Sheets — port and starboard — 4in circ 1 5/16in diam common lay. Standing part secured to ringbolt set in upper main wale aft — reeve through single block on clew to single block secured to ring bolt about 5ft forward of standing part — then forward to fairlead block in bulwark. Belayed to kevel under halfdeck.

 Tacks — port and starboard — 4½in circ 1½in diam tapered to 3in circ 1in diam cabled. Secured to bolt rope loop at clew with a wall-and-crown knot. Reeve from aft forward through chess trees. Belayed to kevel on main rail.

 Clew garnets — port and starboard — 2½in circ 13/16in diam common lay. Standing part timber hitched to yard midway between parrel and yard arm. Reeve through single block at clew to single block secured to yard about 1½ft inboard of standing part to deck. Belayed on main rail under forward shroud.

 Note — Tack, sheet block, and clew garnet block secured in eye of bolt rope with lashing so as to be movable when bonnet is removed.

 Bowlines — port and starboard. Falls — 2¾in circ ⅞in diam common lay. Bridles and cringles — 2½in circ 13/16in diam common lay. Fitted with 3 legs and 2 bullseyes. Falls led forward to single block secured to bowsprit near gammoning. Belayed on forward forecastle rail.

 Buntlines — port, starboard, and centerline — 2in circ ⅝in diam common lay. Standing part secured to foot of sail — led up forward side through single block secured to loop of main stay — to deck on after side. Belayed to cleats or pin rack on mast.

 Note — Buntlines and lowest leg of bowline bridles to be movable from bonnet to alternate position on body of sail.

 Martnets — port and starboard. Upper pendant — 2½in circ 13/16in diam cabled about 6ft long. Upper end — served eye splice over topmast head above shrouds. Lower end — single block for falls seized in with becket.

 Falls — 2in circ ⅝in diam common lay. One end secured to becket of pendant block — reeve through small sheave of fiddle block to pendant block to deck. Belayed on main rail under shrouds. Lower pendant — 2in circ ⅝in diam common lay. Reeve through large sheave of fiddle block with 3 hole deadeye seized in at each end. Deadeye to be same size as for fore topmast shrouds.

 Marnets — 1in circ 5/16in diam common lay. 6 parts spaced along leech on forward and after sides — ends secured to small loops seized to bolt rope. Reeve through deadeyes.

28. FORE COURSE — head about 35½ft — hoist including bonnet about 24ft. Bonnet about 8ft.

Earings — 1¾in circ 7/16in diam common lay.

Robands — braided line — passed through grommets under head rope of sail and tied around yard — spaced about 6in apart.

Sheets — port and starboard — 3½in circ 1⅛in diam common lay. Standing part secured to ringbolt set in upper main wale forward of main channels — reeve through single block on clew to fairlead block in bulwark. Belayed to kevel on main rail.

Tacks — port and starboard — 4in circ 1 5/16in diam tapered to 2½in circ 13/16in diam cabled. Secured to bolt rope loop at clew with a wall-and-crown knot. Reeve through fairlead at outer end of beakhead. Belayed to kevel on forecastle rail under shrouds.

Clew garnets — port and starboard — 2in circ ⅝in diam common lay. Standing part timber hitched to yard midway between parrel and yard arm. Reeve through single block at clew to single block secured to yard about 1½ft inboard of standing part to deck. Belayed on forecastle rail under shrouds.

Note — Tack, sheet block, and clew garnet block secured in eye of bolt rope with lashing so as to be movable when bonnet is removed.

Bowlines — port and starboard. Falls — 2½in circ 13/16in diam common lay. Bridles and cringles — 2¼in circ ¾in diam common lay. Fitted with 3 legs and 2 bullseyes. Falls led forward to single lead block on bowsprit near attachment of forestay. Belayed on forward forecastle rail.

Buntlines — port, starboard, and center line — 1¾in circ 9/16in diam common lay. Standing part secured to foot of sail. Led up forward side through single block secured to loop of forestay — to deck on after side. Belayed to cleats or pin rack on mast.

Note — Buntlines and lowest leg of bowline bridles to be movable from bonnet to alternate position on body of sail.

Martnets — port and starboard. Upper pendant — 2½in circ 13/16in diam cabled about 6ft long. Upper end — served eye splice over topmast head above shrouds. Lower end — single block for falls seized in with becket.

Falls — 2in circ ⅝in diam common lay. One end secured to becket of pendant block — reeve through small sheave of fiddle block to pendant block to deck. Belayed on forecastle rail under shrouds. Lower pendant — 2in circ ⅝in diam common lay. Reeve through large sheave of fiddle block with 3 hole deadeye seized in at each end. Deadeye to be same size as for fore topmast shrouds.

Martnets — 1in circ 5/16in diam common lay. 6 parts spaced along leech on forward and after sides — ends secured to small loops seized to bolt rope. Reeve through deadeyes.

29. MAIN TOPSAIL — head about 18½ft — foot about 46½ft — hoist about 28ft.

Earings — 1¼in circ 7/16in diam common lay.

Robands — braided line — passed through grommets under head rope of sail and tied around yard — spaced about 6in apart.

THE MAYFLOWER

Sheets — port and starboard — 4in circ 1 5/16in diam common lay. Secured to eye of bolt rope at clew with a wall-and-crown knot. Reeve through single block at lower yard arm to single block secured to lower yard near ties. Belayed to cleat on mast at deck.

Clewlines — port and starboard — 2in circ ⅝in diam common lay. Standing part timber hitched to yard near tie. Reeve through single block at clew to single block secured to yard inboard of standing part — then through hole in main top and fairlead trucks on shrouds. Belayed on halfdeck rail under shrouds.

Bowlines — port and starboard — Falls 2¼in circ ¾in diam common lay. Bridles and cringles — 2in circ ⅝in diam common lay. Fitted with 4 legs and 3 bullseyes. Falls led forward through single lead block attached to main topmast stay by short pendant to double block strapped to foremast below fore top. Belayed on after forecastle rail.

Leechlines — port and starboard — 2¼in circ ¾in diam common lay. Standing part secured to leech of sail — reeve up forward side to single block secured to tie just above yard — to deck on after side through hole in main top and fairlead trucks on shrouds. Belayed on halfdeck rail under shrouds.

30. FORE TOPSAIL — head about 14ft — foot about 35ft — hoist about 24½ft. Earings — 1in circ 5/16in diam common lay.

Robands — braided line — passed through grommets under head rope of sail and tied around yard — spaced about 6in apart.

Sheets — port and starboard — 3½in circ 1⅛in diam common lay. Secured to eye of bolt rope at clew with a wall-and-crown knot. Reeve through single block at lower yard arm to single block secured to lower yard near ties. Belayed to cleat on mast at deck.

Clewlines — port and starboard — 2in circ ⅝in diam common lay. Standing part timber hitched to yard near tie. Reeve through single block at clew to single block secured to yard inboard of standing part — then through hole in fore top and fairlead trucks on shrouds. Belayed on forecastle rail under shrouds.

Bowlines — port and starboard — Falls — 2in circ ⅝in diam common lay. Bridles and cringles — 1½in circ ½in diam common lay. Fitted with 3 legs and 2 bullseyes. Falls led forward to single lead block attached to fore topmast stay by short pendant to single lead block secured to bowsprit forward of forestay collar. Belayed on forward forecastle rail.

Leechlines — port and starboard — 2¼in circ ¾in diam common lay. Standing part secured to leech of sail — reeve up forward side to single block secured to tie just above yard — to deck on after side through hole in fore top and fairlead trucks on shrouds. Belayed on forecastle rail under shrouds.

31. SPRITSAIL — head about 25½ft — hoist about 18ft. Earings — 1⅛in circ ⅜in diam common lay.

Robands — braided line — passed through grommets under head rope of sail and tied around yard — spaced about 6in apart.

Sheets — port and starboard. Pendant — 4in circ 1 5/16in diam cabled — about 35ft long. One end secured to eye of bolt rope at clew with a wall-and-crown knot — single block for falls spliced or seized in other end.

Falls — 3¼in circ 1 1/16in diam common lay. Standing part secured to same ringbolt as fore sheet — reeve through pendant block to fairlead block in bulwark. Belayed to kevel on main rail.

Clewlines — port and starboard — 2¼in circ ¾in diam common lay. Standing part secured to clew of sail — reeve through single block secured to yard midway between parrel and yard arm (at garnet block). Belayed on forward forecastle rail.

Buntline — centerline only — 2¼in circ ¾in diam common lay. Standing part secured to foot of sail — led up forward side to single lead block on bowsprit. Belayed on forward forecastle rail.

32. MIZZEN (LATEEN) — about 37ft along yard — leech including bonnet about 30ft — foot of bonnet about 33ft. Bonnet about 6½ft deep.

Earings — 1⅛in circ ⅜in diam common lay.

Robands — braided line — passed through grommets under head rope of sail and tied around yard — spaced about 6in apart.

Sheet — 2¼in circ ¾in diam common lay. Standing part secured to becket of single block on outrigger — reeve through single block on clew to outrigger block. Belayed to cleat on centerline rail stanchion on poop deck.

Tack — 3in circ 1in diam common lay. Standing part secured to eye of bonnet bolt rope at clew with a wall-and-crown knot. Hitched to suitable timber head when in use.

Brails — port and starboard. Falls — 1½in circ ½in diam common lay. Cringle — 1⅛in circ ⅜in diam common lay. Fitted with 2 legs and one bullseye. Standing part of falls secured to bullseye — reeve through single block secured to yard below parrel. Belayed on half deck rail. Cringles secured to loops attached to bolt rope — alternate positions on bonnet and main body of sail.

Martnets — port and starboard. Falls — 1½in circ ½in diam common lay. Legs — 1in circ 5/16in diam common lay. One end of falls to have 3 hole deadeye seized in — deadeye to be same size as for fore topmast shrouds. Reeve through double block at mizzen masthead. Belayed on halfdeck rail. Legs in 6 parts spaced along leech — end secured to small loops secured to bolt rope. Reeve through deadeyes.

33. FLAG HALYARDS — fore-, main- and mizzenmasts — port and starboard. 1in circ 5/16in diam common lay. Reeve through sheaves in flagstaff trucks. Belayed in convenient locations.

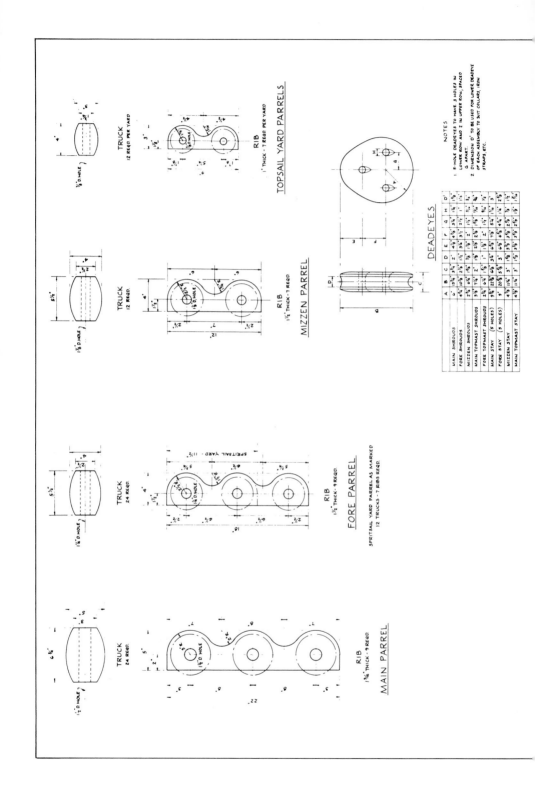

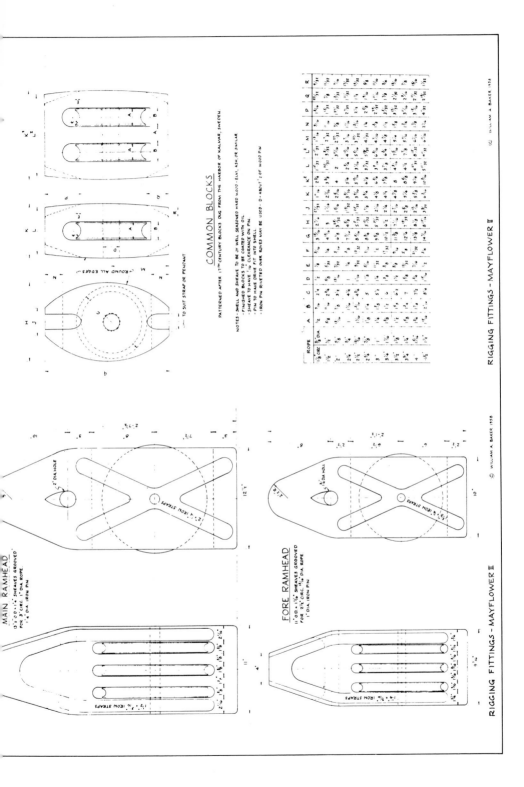

COMMON BLOCKS

PATTERNED AFTER 17TH CENTURY BLOCKS DUG FROM THE HARBOR OF KALMAR, SWEDEN.

NOTES - SHELL AND SHEAVE TO BE OF WELL SEASONED HARD WOOD - ELM, ASH, OR SIMILAR.
- FINISHED BLOCKS TO BE COATED WITH OIL.
- SHEAVE TO HAVE 1/16 CLEARANCE ON PIN.
- PIN TO HAVE DRIVE FIT INTO SHELL.
- IRON PIN RIVETED OVER ROVES MAY BE USED - D - ABOUT 1/2 OF WOOD PIN.

RIGGING FITTINGS - MAYFLOWER II

© WILLIAM A. BAKER 1958

MAIN RAMHEAD

13' O.D. x 14" SHEAVES GROOVED
FOR 3" CIRC. 1" DIA. ROPE
1/4" DIA. IRON PIN

FORE RAMHEAD

11" O.D. x 1⅛" SHEAVES GROOVED
FOR 2¼" CIRC. 1½" DIA. ROPE
1" DIA. IRON PIN

RIGGING FITTINGS - MAYFLOWER II

© WILLIAM A. BAKER 1958

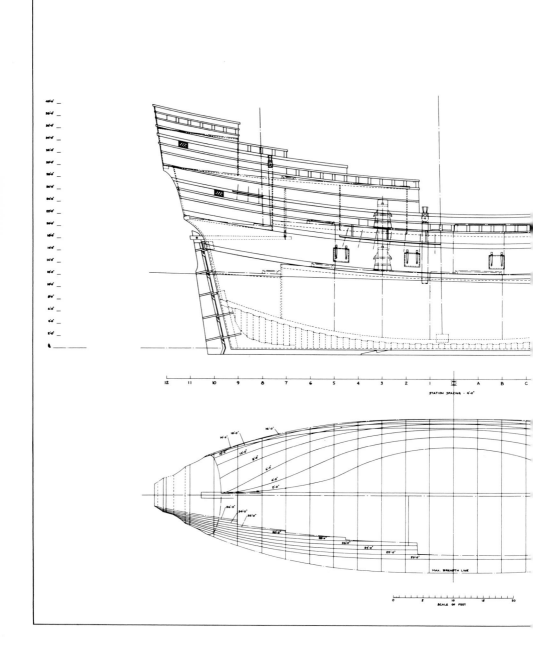

STATION SPACING - 4'-0"

MAX. BREADTH LINE

SCALE OF FEET

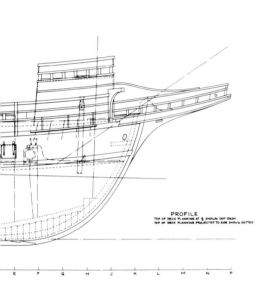

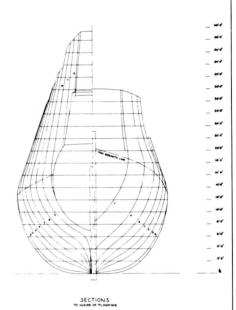

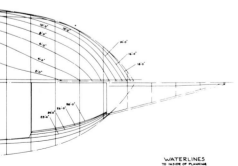

PROFILE
TOP OF DECK PLANKING AT ℄ SHOWN DOT-DASH
TOP OF DECK PLANKING PROJECTED TO SIDE SHOWN DOTTED

E   F   G   H   J   K   L   M   N   P

SECTIONS
TO INSIDE OF PLANKING

WATERLINES
TO INSIDE OF PLANKING

LENGTH OF KEEL	58'-0"
BREADTH TO INSIDE OF PLANK	25'-0"
DEPTH - TOP OF KEEL TO THE BREADTH	12'-6"
BURDEN BY RULE OF 1582	181 TONS

THE NEW
MAYFLOWER

BUILT BY
J.W. & A. UPHAM, LTD.
BRIXHAM, DEVON, ENGLAND
1955-1957

DESIGNED BY
William A. Baker
NAVAL ARCHITECT
HINGHAM   MASS.

PLAN A - PROFILE, SECTIONS & WATERLINES

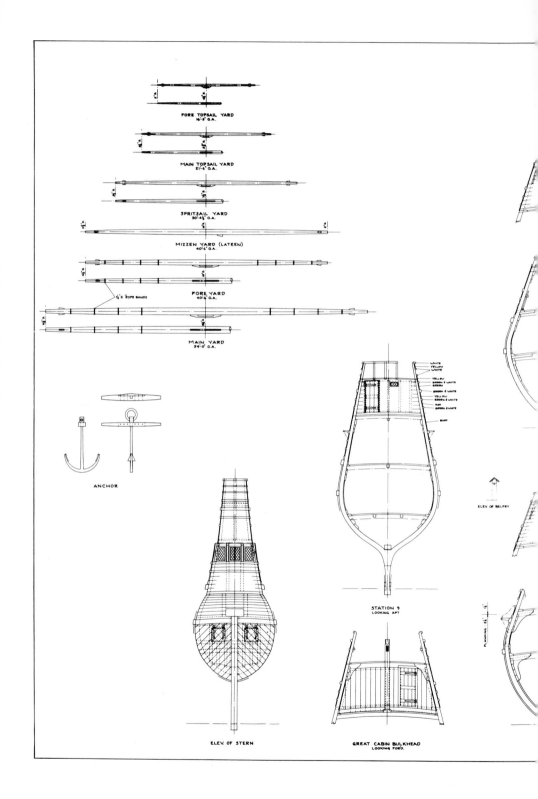

FORE TOPSAIL YARD
16'-5" O.A.

MAIN TOPSAIL YARD
21'-6" O.A.

SPRITSAIL YARD
30'-4½" O.A.

MIZZEN YARD (LATEEN)
40'-6" O.A.

FORE YARD
40'-0" O.A.

1½" D. ROPE BANDS

MAIN YARD
54'-0" O.A.

ANCHOR

ELEV. OF STERN

STATION 9
LOOKING AFT

GREAT CABIN BULKHEAD
LOOKING FOR'D.

WHITE
YELLOW
WHITE

YELLOW
GREEN & WHITE
GREEN

GREEN & WHITE
YELLOW
GREEN & WHITE

RED
GREEN & WHITE

BUFF

ELEV. OF BELFRY

PLANKING

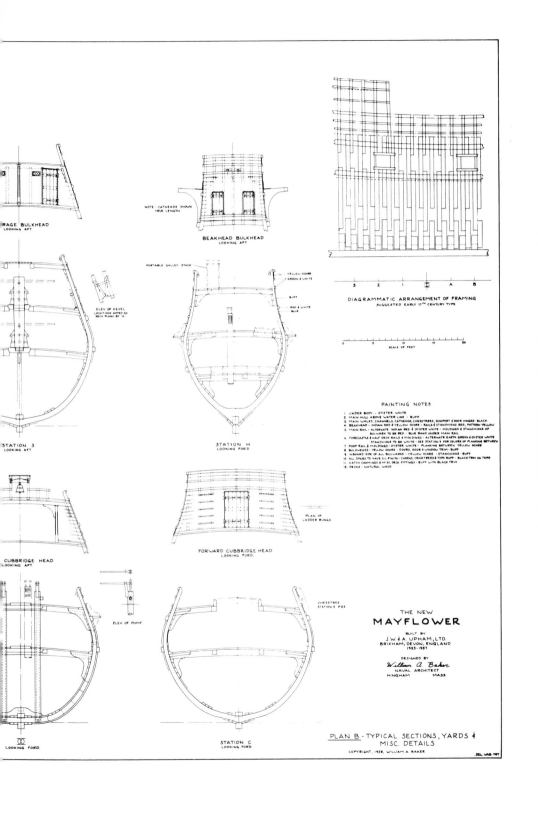

RAGE BULKHEAD
LOOKING AFT

BEAKHEAD BULKHEAD
LOOKING AFT

NOTE · CATHEADS SHOWN
TRUE LENGTH

DIAGRAMMATIC ARRANGEMENT OF FRAMING
SUGGESTED EARLY 17TH CENTURY TYPE

PORTABLE GALLEY STACK

YELLOW OCHRE
GREEN & WHITE

BUFF

RED & WHITE
BLUE

ELEV. OF KEVEL
LOCATIONS NOTED ON
DECK PLANS BY "K"

STATION 3
LOOKING AFT

STATION H
LOOKING FORD.

SCALE OF FEET

PAINTING NOTES

1. UNDER BODY - OYSTER WHITE
2. MAIN HULL ABOVE WATER LINE - BUFF
3. MAIN WALES, CHANNELS, CATHEADS, CHESSTREES, GUNPORT & DOOR HINGES· BLACK
4. BEAKHEAD - INDIAN RED & YELLOW OCHRE - RAILS & STANCHIONS RED, PATTERN YELLOW
5. MAIN RAIL - ALTERNATE INDIAN RED & OYSTER WHITE - MOLDINGS & STANCHIONS OF
   BULWARK TO BE RED - BLUE BAND UNDER MAIN RAIL
6. FORECASTLE & HALF DECK RAILS & MOLDINGS - ALTERNATE EARTH GREEN & OYSTER WHITE
   STANCHIONS TO BE WHITE - SEE STATION 5 FOR COLORS OF PLANKING BETWEEN
7. POOP RAIL & MOLDINGS - OYSTER WHITE - PLANKING BETWEEN - YELLOW OCHRE
8. BULKHEADS - YELLOW OCHRE - DOORS, DOOR & WINDOW TRIM - BUFF
9. INBOARD SIDE OF ALL BULWARKS - YELLOW OCHRE - STANCHIONS · BUFF
10. ALL SPARS TO HAVE OIL FINISH - CHEEKS, CROSSTREES & TOPS BUFF - BLACK TRIM ON TOPS
11. HATCH COAMINGS & MISC DECK FITTINGS - BUFF WITH BLACK TRIM
12. DECKS - NATURAL WOOD

CUBBRIDGE HEAD
LOOKING AFT

ELEV. OF PUMP

PLAN OF
LADDER RUNGS

FORWARD CUBBRIDGE HEAD
LOOKING FORD.

CHESSTREE
STATION E P.43

THE NEW
MAYFLOWER

BUILT BY
J.W. & A. UPHAM, LTD.
BRIXHAM, DEVON, ENGLAND
1955-1957

DESIGNED BY
William A. Baker
NAVAL ARCHITECT
HINGHAM   MASS.

LOOKING FORD.

STATION C
LOOKING FORD.

PLAN B - TYPICAL SECTIONS, YARDS &
MISC. DETAILS

COPYRIGHT, 1958, WILLIAM A. BAKER

DEL. W.A.B. 1957

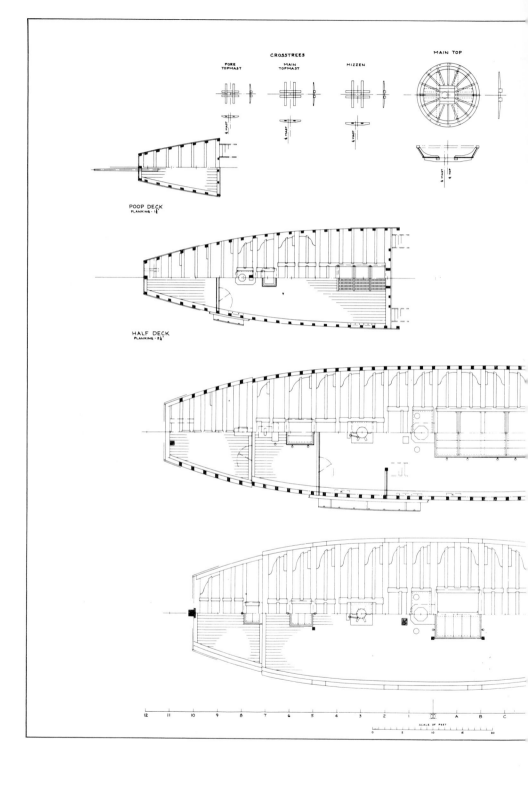

CROSSTREES

FORE TOPMAST MAIN TOPMAST MIZZEN MAIN TOP

POOP DECK
PLANKING - 1½"

HALF DECK
PLANKING - 2½"

12 11 10 9 8 7 6 5 4 3 2 1 A B C

SCALE OF FEET
0 5 10 15 20

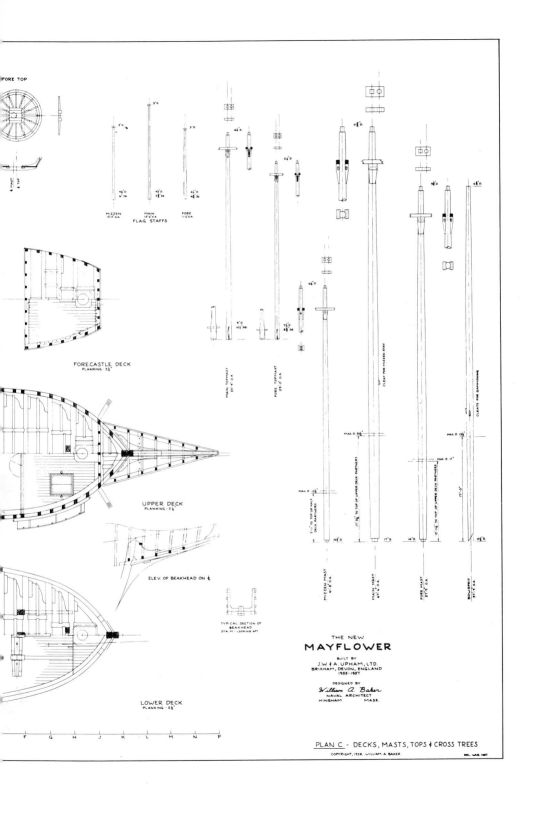

FORE TOP

FORECASTLE DECK
PLANKING · 2½"

UPPER DECK
PLANKING · 2½"

ELEV. OF BEAKHEAD ON ℄

TYPICAL SECTION OF
BEAKHEAD
STA. M · LOOKING AFT

LOWER DECK
PLANKING · 2½"

MIZZEN
13'-0 O.A.

MAIN
13'-6 O.A.

FORE
11'-6 O.A.

FLAG STAFFS

MAIN TOPMAST
33'-1 O.A.

FORE TOPMAST
29'-0 O.A.

MIZZEN MAST
41'-8 O.A.

MAIN MAST
67'-6 O.A.

FORE MAST
57'-9 O.A.

BOWSPRIT
37'-9 O.A.

CLEAT FOR MIZZEN STAY

CLEATS FOR GAMMONING

THE NEW
MAYFLOWER

BUILT BY
J.W. & A. UPHAM, LTD.
BRIXHAM, DEVON, ENGLAND
1955-1957

DESIGNED BY
William A. Baker
NAVAL ARCHITECT
HINGHAM   MASS.

PLAN C - DECKS, MASTS, TOPS & CROSS TREES

DEL. W.A.B. 1957

NOTES

Chapter 1 *Seventeenth-Century Naval Architecture*
A. GENERAL
For detailed discussions of the development of ships through the centuries any of the following may be consulted:
Anderson, R C and Romola, *The Sailing Ship* (New York, 1947).
Chatterton, E Keble, *Sailing Ships and Their Story* (Philadelphia, 1923).
Chatterton, E Keble, *Ships and Ways of Other Days* (London, 1913).
Clowes, G S Laird, *Sailing Ships* (London, 1932).
B. RIG
1. Laughton, L G C, 'Crayers and Hoys', *The Mariner's Mirror*, 27 (1941), 341–2.
2. Phelps Stokes print collections of the New York Public Library.
3. Mainwaring, Sir Henry, 'The Seaman's Dictionary' in Mainwaring, G E, and Perrin, W G, *The Life and Works of Sir Henry Mainwaring* (London, 1922) 2, 120.

    For a complete treatise on the rigging of seventeenth-century ships see Anderson, R C, *Seventeenth-Century Rigging* (London, 1955).
C. FORM AND CONSTRUCTION
4. Mathew Baker's Notebook, Pepys 2820, Magdalene College Library. By courtesy of the Master and Fellows of Magdalene College, Cambridge, England. Hereafter referred to as the Baker MS.
5. Salisbury, W, 'Early Tonnage Measurement in England', *The Mariner's Mirror* 52 (1966), 41–51; 'Rules for Ships Built For, and Hired By, the Navy', *The Mariner's Mirror* 52, 173–80; 'Early Tonnage Measurement in England, Part III. HM Customs, and Statutory Rules', *The Mariner's Mirror* 52, 329–40; 'Early Tonnage Measurement in England, Part IV. Rules Used by Shipwrights, and Merchants', *The Mariner's Mirror* 53 (1967), 251–64.
6. Salisbury, W, and Anderson, R C, *A Treatise on Shipbuilding and A Treatise on Rigging Written About 1620–1625* (London, 1958).
7. Raleigh, Sir Walter, *Judicious and Select Essays and Observations* (London, 1650).
8. Salisbury, W, 'The Framing of Models', *The Mariner's Mirror*, 40 (1954), 156–9.

Chapter 2 *Early Colonists — The* Mayflower
B. HISTORY
1. Bradford, William, *Of Plimoth Plantation*, printed by order of the General Court (Boston, 1899).
2. Hutchinson, J R, 'The *Mayflower*, Her Identity and Tonnage', *New England Historical and Genealogical Register*, 70 (1916), 337–42.

NOTES

3. Marsden, R G, 'The *Mayflower*', *The Mayflower Descendant*, 18 (1916), 1–13.

4. Mourt, G (Bradford, William, and Winslow, Edward), *A Relation, or Journall of the Beginnings and Proceedings of the English Plantation settled at Plimoth, in New England* (London, 1622).

5. Horrocks, J W, 'The *Mayflower*', *The Mariner's Mirror*, 8 (1922). A long article in several parts; Anderson, R C, 'Have the *Mayflower*'s Masts Been Found?', *The Mariner's Mirror*, 19 (1933), 164–71.

6. Bradford, General Court Edition, 92.

7. Bradford, William, *A History of Plymouth Plantation 1620–1647* (Boston, 1912), 148.

8. Oppenheim, M, *A History of the Administration of the Royal Navy and of Merchant Shipping in Relation to the Navy* (London and New York, 1896), 126.

9. Padfield, Peter, *The Sea is a Magic Carpet* (London, 1959), 16.

10. For a full discussion of the subject see Baker, William A, 'Deck Heights in the Early Seventeenth Century', *The American Neptune*, 22 (1962), 99–105.

11. Anonymous MS, *A Treatise on Rigging*, Occasional Publications No 1, The Society for Nautical Research (London, 1921).

12. Anderson, R C, *The Rigging of Ships in the Days of the Spritsail Topmast, 1600–1720* (Salem, 1927). A revision titled *Seventeenth Century Rigging* was published in London in 1955.

13. Miller, Thomas, *The Complete Modellist* (London, 1667).

14. Moore, Sir Alan, 'Rigging in the Seventeenth Century', *The Mariner's Mirror*, 2 (1912), 267–74; 3 (1913), 7–13, 328–36; 4 (1914), 260–65.

15. Griffith Baily Coale, 'Arrival of the First Permanent English Settlers off Jamestown, Virginia, 13 May 1607', *The American Neptune*, 10 (1950), 9.

Chapter 3 *Small Craft — the Pilgrims' Shallop*

1. Smith, Captain John, *The Adventures and Discourses of Captain John Smith* (London, Paris, and New York, 1883), 81.

2. Mourt, G (Bradford, William, and Winslow, Edward). *A Relation, or Journall of the Beginnings and Proceedings of the English Plantation settled at Plimoth, in New England* (London, 1622).

3. A plan showing my ideas concerning this shallop may be obtained from the Old Dartmouth Historical Society, 18 Johnny Cake Hill, New Bedford, Massachusetts, USA, 02740.

4. Saltonstall, William G, *Ports of Piscataqua* (Cambridge, Mass, 1941), 10.

5. For more information on colonial shallops and their descendants see: Baker, William A, *Sloops & Shallops* (Barre, 1966) and Chapelle, Howard I, *American Small Sailing Craft* (New York, 1951).

THE MAYFLOWER

Chapter 4 *On Pinnaces*

1. Bradford, William, *Of Plimoth Plantation* (Boston, 1899), 253.
2. Hakluyt, Richard, *The Principal Navigations, Voyages, Traffiques & Discoveries of the English Nation* (London and New York, 1907), 5, 309–17.
3. Oppenheim, M, *A History of the Administration of the Royal Navy . . .* (London and New York, 1896), 255–6.
4. Coale, Griffith Baily, 'Arrival of the First Permanent English Settlers off Jamestown, Virginia, 13 May 1607', *The American Neptune*, 10 (1950), 5–14; Fee, Robert G C, 'The 1957 Jamestown Fleet', *The American Neptune*, 17 (1957), 173–80.
5. Brewington, Marion V, 'What the Designs Show', *Maryland Historical Magazine*, 18 (1953), 189–90.
6. Purchas, Samuel, *Hakluytas Posthumus or Purchas his Pilgrimmes* (Glasgow, 1906) XIX, 39–41.
7. Cannenburg, W Voobeijtel, *Beschrijvende Catalogus* (Amsterdam, 1943), Plaat 3.

Chapter 5 *A Coastal Trader — A Colonial Bark circa 1640*

1. Bruce, R Stuart, 'Barkalongen', *The Mariner's Mirror*, 4 (1914), 127.
2. Andrews, K R, 'Appraisements of Elizabethan Privateersmen', *The Mariner's Mirror*, 37 (1951), 76–9.
3. McGrath, Patrick V, 'The Merchant Venturers and Bristol Shipping in the Early Seventeenth Century', *The Mariner's Mirror*, 36 (1950), 69, 74.
4. Lechford, Thomas, 'Plain Dealing or News from New England', *Massachusetts Historical Society Collections, Series 3*, 3 (1833), 101; Robinson, John, and Dow, G F, *The Sailing Ships of New England, 1607–1907* (Salem, 1922), 12.
5. Robinson and Dow, 13.
6. Morris, E P, *The Fore-and-Aft Rig in America* (New Haven, 1927), 7.
7. Winthrop, John, *History of New England* (New York, 1959), 165.
8. Bradford, William, *Of Plimoth Plantation* (Boston, 1899), 318.
9. Winthrop, *op cit*, 66.
10. *Ibid*, 156.
11. Forbes, A B, Editor, *Records of the Suffolk County Court* (Boston, 1933), 29, 135.
12. Holman, Richard B, 'John Foster's Woodcut Map of New England', *Paga*, 8 (1960), 53–93.
13. Massachusetts Archives, *Commercial*, 7 (1685–1714), 400.
14. Szymanski, H, 'The Snow', *The Mariner's Mirror*, 9 (1923), 121.

Chapter 6 *The Colonial Ketch*

1. Bradford, William, *Of Plimoth Plantation* (Boston, 1899), 202–3.

NOTES

2. Robinson, John, and Dow, G F, *The Sailing Ships of New England, 1607–1907* (Salem, 1922), 23.

3. White, E W, *British Fishing-Boats and Coastal Craft* (London, 1950) Part I – Historical Survey.

4. These four quotations are given under *Catch* in *A New English Dictionary on Historical Principles* (Oxford).

5. Smith, David B, 'The Nomenclature of the Thames', *The Mariner's Mirror*, 2 (1912), 342.

6. Laughton, L G Carr, 'Crayers and Hoys', *The Mariner's Mirror*, 27 (1941), 342.

7. Nance, R M, 'Ketches', *The Mariner's Mirror*, 2 (1912), 362.

8. Leslie, R C, *Old Sea Wings, Ways, and Words* (London, 1930) [3]–[4].

9. *Ibid*, [5].

10. AM, 'Hoy, Ketch, Barque', *The Mariner's Mirror*, 5 (1919), 154–5.

11. Laughton, L G Carr, 'Ketch Rig', *The Mariner's Mirror*, 43 (1957), 169.

12. Massachusetts Archives, *Commercial*, vol 7.

13. Benham, Hervey, *Once Upon a Tide* (London, 1955), 47–8.

14. Laughton, L G Carr, 'Ketch Yachts', *The Mariner's Mirror*, 18 (1932), 197–8.

15. Dow, G F, Editor, *Records and Files of the Quarterly Courts of Essex County, Massachusetts* (Salem, 1912), 3, 334–5.

16. Essex County Quarterly Court Files, 30, 131.

17. Casson, Lionel, 'The Sprit-Rig in the Ancient World', *The Mariner's Mirror*, 46 (1960), 16.

18. HHB, 'Early Sprit-sail', *The Mariner's Mirror*, 6 (1920), 248.

19. RMN, 'Smack-sails, XV Century', *The Mariner's Mirror*, 6 (1920), 343–4.

20. Massachusetts Historical Society, *Winthrop Papers* (Boston, 1943), 49.

21. Young, Alexander, *Chronicles of the First Planters of the Colony of Massachusetts Bay from 1623 to 1636* (Boston, 1846), 185, 323.

22. Winthrop, John, *History of New England* (New York, 1929), 334.

23. Beck, Horace P, *The American Indian as a Sea-Fighter in Colonial Times* (Mystic, 1959), 27–8.

24. Chapelle, Howard I, 'The Origin of the Marconi Rig', *The American Neptune*, 20 (1960), 65–6.

25. Anderson, R C, 'Early Royal Yachts', *The Mariner's Mirror*, 9 (1923), 250.

GLOSSARY

abaft — back of, behind

batten — a thin strip of wood used by ship's carpenters to reproduce the curves or irregular lines of a vessel's hull

beak (*beakhead*) — in the seventeenth century the decorative construction at the bow of a ship

beam — width of ship

becket — a loop formed in the rope strapping of a block at the bottom, to which another rope may be secured

bilge — rounded part of the hull between the side and bottom either inside or outside of the hull

block — a pulley or sheave, or set of pulleys, in a frame or shell

bluff bowed — a vessel having a blunt, full or broad forward end

bonaventure mizzen — the second mizzen mast on four-masted ships of the late sixteenth and early seventeenth centuries

bonnet — additional piece of canvas laced to the foot of a sail

boom — a spar used to stretch the foot of a fore-and-aft sail

bow — the forward end of a vessel

bowlines — ropes used to extend the windward edges of square sails tight forward and steady

bowsprit — a spar projecting forward of the stem, inclined slightly upward

bridles — short ropes each end of which is secured to the vertical edges of a square sail, to which the bowlines are fixed

bulkhead — a vertical partition corresponding to the wall of a building

bulwark — the ship's side above a deck; or the top sides of a vessel which extend above the deck like a fence

burden (*burthen*) — the carrying capacity of a vessel; also the weight of the cargo

buttocks — a curved line or vertical section of a vessel's hull in profile

carvel planking — smooth seamed planking

ceiling — inside planking or skin of a vessel

clew — either lower corner of a square sail and the lower after corner of a fore-and-aft sail

to clew up — to haul the lower corner or corners of a sail up to a gaff or yard by means of clew lines

clinker-built — lapped strakes of planking

coaming — raised boundary of a hatch, skylight, etc

course — lowest square sail on any mast of a square-rigged ship

cringles — small loops made on the bolt-rope of a sail to which the bowline bridles are secured

cross sail — a sail set athwartship, a square sail

GLOSSARY

crosstrees — short, flat pieces of timber let in and bolted athwartship to trestle-trees at the masthead to support the tops, etc

deadeye — small hardwood block without sheave, containing 3 or more holes and with groove cut around outside to receive a strop; part of the rigging used for securing shrouds to chain plates

double-ender — a vessel having its bow and stern of the same shape – pointed, rounded, etc

earings — small ropes employed to fasten the upper corners of sails to yards or other spars

eyes (of the boat) — extreme bow of the vessel

fair — smooth without abruptness or unevenness

falls (tackle) — the rope that connects the two blocks of a tackle

fidded — topmast supported by square bar resting on trestle trees

floor (ship) — the bottom of a ship extending from the keel out to the turn of the bilge

fore-and-aft sails — triangular or rectangular sails carried in a fore-and-aft direction and secured on their forward side to a stay or mast

forecastle — the superstructure at the bow – traditionally the location of the crew's quarters

forefoot — the junction of the keel and stem

freeboard — vertical distance from upper or watertight deck to the waterline or surface of the water

futtock — the frame timber being an extension of the floor up to and around the bilge to the top timber

gaff — a spar used along the head of a fore-and-aft sail

halyard — ropes or tackle used for hoisting or lowering sails, booms and other top gear of a vessel

heel — the lower end of a tree, timber, mast, or the inner end of a boom; after end of a ship's keel; outside angle of a knee

helm (tiller) — the lever by which the rudder is directed

hounds — a name given to those parts of a masthead which gradually project on each side from the cylindrical shape of the mast. The hounds support the trestle-trees, the topmast, and the rigging of the lower mast

jib — common term for a triangular sail carried on a stay ahead of the fore-mast

keel — the backbone of the ship

keelson (kelson) — an auxiliary keel or stringer built over the frames on the inside of the hull extending along, over and parallel to the keel

kevels — small pieces of timber secured to the rail stanchions to which various halyards, sheets and tacks are belayed

knee — an angular piece of timber – usually a natural crook used to strengthen corners – used mainly to secure deck beams to a vessel's sides. Hanging knees are set in vertical plane while lodging knees are set horizontally *lanyard* — pieces of light rope passing through deadeyes to tighten and secure shrouds and stays

larboard — see *port*

lateen sail — a triangular sail extended by a long tapering yard, slung at about one-third the distance from the lower end which is brought down to the deck

leeboard — a flat board let down vertically into the water on the lee side of a ship or boat to prevent leeward motion

lines — the plan of a ship that shows its form

load waterline — the line representing the surface of the water when the ship is loaded with her stores and cargo – and guns and ammunition, if she is an armed vessel

lug (*rig*) — a quadrilateral sail bent upon a yard that crosses the mast obliquely

martnet — an assemblage of deadeyes and ropes having six legs which gathers the side of a course up to its yard

mast — a long cylindrical piece of timber, to which are fastened the yards, sails, and rigging. On large vessels, each mast is composed of several sections – the lower mast, topmast, topgallant mast, etc

midship bend — the main frame of a ship

mizzenmast — the after mast on a three masted vessel

mold — a pattern or template of a part of a vessel's frame, structure, etc, usually made of thin wood battens or boards

parrel — an assemblage of vertical wooden bars called 'ribs' and heavy wooden balls called 'trucks' all threaded on and bound by a rope around a mast and used to secure a yard to the mast

pendant — a stout rope with a tackle attached to one end which serves to transmit the power of its tackle to some other object

poop — the raised after portion of the vessel above the upper or quarter deck

port (*direction*) — left-hand side of a vessel when looking from aft forward

purchase — a tackle frequently employed in fixing or extending the rigging of a ship

rabbet — a depression or channel in a piece of timber cut for the purpose of receiving and securing the edge and hood ends of bottom and side planking

rake — the overhang of the stem or stern beyond the perpendicular to the keel; any part or thing that forms an obtuse angle with the horizon: eg rake of the mast

ratlines — short lengths of tarred line seized with a clove-hitch across the shrouds about 14in apart, parallel with the sheer poles or decks – used by crew for ascending or descending from aloft

reach — to sail with the wind within a few points of abeam

reef — part of a sail rolled and tied down to reduce area exposed to the wind

rig — the arrangement of masts, spars and sails on a boat or ship

rigging — a general name given to all the ropes employed to support the masts and to extend or reduce the sails

GLOSSARY

robands — bands or lines used to secure a sail to a spar

scantlings — a general term referring to the hull structure of a vessel

scarf (scarph) — the lapped joint connecting two timbers or planks together

section — the curved line shown by a vertical plane cutting a vessel athwartships

sheave — the wheel or pulley in the mortise of a tackle block over which the rope runs

sheer — fore-and-aft curvature of a deck

sheet — a rope controlling the after lower corner of a sail

shroud — heavy ropes which brace the mast athwartships

spar — a long round or oval timber, as a mast, yard, boom or gaff

sprit — a small staff or spar used on some fore-and-aft sails which extends diagonally from the mast across the sail to support the peak

starboard — right-hand side of a ship when looking from aft forward

stays — strong ropes, to support the masts forward, which extend from their upper part, at the masthead, toward the fore part of the ship

staysail — any sail hoisted on a stay, as a triangular sail between two masts

steeve — to incline upward at an angle

stem — a heavy timber forming the extreme bow of a ship extending from the keel to the forecastle deck

stepping (mast) — fitting lower end of the mast in a wooden socket

stern — the after end of a vessel

sternpost — a wooden piece secured at its lower end to the after end of a keel – the upper end supporting the transom

strake — a continuous breadth of planking or ceiling running from stempost to sternpost on the ship's frame

to tack — to proceed to windward by a series of courses as close to the wind as the vessel will sail

tack — the lower forward corner of a sail – also the rope used to secure it

tackle — a hoisting or moving contrivance of ropes and blocks for managing sails and spars or moving heavy weights

thwart — the cross seat in an open boat

ton; tun; tonnage — a measure of the internal capacity of a vessel (see *burden*)

topgallant mast — see *mast*

topsides — the sides of a ship above the waterline

train oil — oil tried out from fat of whales (blackfish)

transom — the athwartship timber, structure or frame at the after end of a vessel's hull framing

traverse board — seventeenth century navigation aid – used for recording the time sailed on various courses

trestle trees — two strong pieces of timber, bolted to the sides of a masthead, to support the crosstrees, top, and weight of the mast above (see *crosstrees*) *tumblehome* — the sloping in of the vessel's topsides above the point of greatest beam

treenails — round or octagonal pieces of hardwood driven through the frames, timbers, and planking of a vessel to fasten or connect them together

waist cloth — heavy cloths hung along the sides of seventeenth-century ships to conceal the crew when in battle

wale — a thick strake of outside planking worked in along the sides of a vessel about midway between the plank sheer and the light waterline for stiffening

weather deck — an upper deck with no overhead protection

whole-molding — a system of designing, used mainly for small boats, whereby all the transverse sections are drawn with only two molds

windlass — a mechanical device used to hoist anchors

yard — a horizontal athwartship spar fitted to the forward side of the mast on a sailing vessel – used to support square sails

BIBLIOGRAPHY

BOOKS

Anderson, R C, *The Rigging of Ships in the Days of the Spritsail Topmast, 1600-1720* (Salem, 1927; reprinted London, 1982).

Anderson, R C, *Seventeenth-Century Rigging* (London, 1955).

Anderson, R C and Romola, *The Sailing Ship* (New York, 1947).

Aubin, —, *Dictionaire de Marine* (Amsterdam, 1702).

Baker, William A, *Sloops & Shallops* (Barre, 1966).

Beck, Horace P, *The American Indian as a Sea-fighter in Colonial Times* (Mystic, 1959).

Benham, Hervey, *Once Upon a Tide* (London, 1955).

Bradford, William, *Of Plimoth Plantation*, General Court Edition (Boston, 1899).

Bradford, William, *Of Plimoth Plantation*, Massachusetts Historical Society Edition (Boston, 1912).

Cannenburg, W Voorbeijtel, *Beschrijvende Catalogus* (Amsterdam, 1943).

Chapelle, Howard I, *American Small Sailing Craft* (New York, 1951).

Chatterton, E Keble, *Ships and Ways of Other Days* (London, 1913).

Chatterton, E Keble, *Sailing Ships and Their Story* (Philadelphia, 1923).

Clowes, G S Laird, *Sailing Ships* (London, 1932).

Cotgrave, Randle, *A Dictionarie of the French and English Tongues* (London, 1611).

Dassie, le Sieur, *L'Architecture Navale* (Paris, 1677).

Dow, G F, Editor, *Records and Files of the Quarterly Courts of Essex County, Massachusetts* (Salem, 1912).

Forbes, A B, Editor, *Records of the Suffolk County Court* (Boston, 1933).

Guillet, le Sieur, *Dictionaire du Gentilhomme* (The Hague, 1686).

Hakluyt, Richard, *The Principal Navigations, Voyages, Traffiques & Discoveries of the English Nation* (London and New York, 1907).

Harris, John, *Lexicon Technicum* (London, 1704).

Hubbard, Reverend Williams, *A Narrative of the Trouble with the Indians in New England* (Boston, 1677).

Leslie, R C, *Old Sea Wings, Ways, and Words* (London, 1930).

Mainwaring, Sir Henry, 'The Seaman's Dictionary' in Mainwaring, G E, and Perrin, W G, *The Life and Works of Sir Henry Mainwaring* (London, 1922).

Massachusetts Historical Society, *Winthrop Papers* (Boston, 1943).

Miller, Thomas, *The Complete Modellist* (London, 1667).

Morris, E P, *The Fore-and-Aft Rig in America* (New Haven, 1927).

Mourt, G (Bradford, William, and Winslow, Edward). *A Relation, or Journall, of the Beginnings and Proceedings of the English Plantation settled at Plimoth, in New England* (London, 1622).

179